Theolog...

Theology against the Nuclear Horizon

Edited by Alan Race

SCM PRESS LTD

261.85

British Library Cataloguing in Publication Data

Theology against the nuclear horizon.
1. Nuclear power – Christian viewpoints
I. Race, Alan
261.8'5

ISBN 0-334-02349-1

20029312

First published 1988
by SCM Press Ltd
26–30 Tottenham Road, London N1 4BZ

Typeset at The Spartan Press Ltd, Lymington
and printed in Great Britain by
The Camelot Press Plc, Southampton.

We looked to God for absolute security, and found a mystery which we can only take on trust.

Dorothy Rowe, *Living with the Bomb*

Extinction is not something to contemplate, it is something to rebel against.

Jonathan Schell, *The Fate of the Earth*

Acknowledgments

I should like to thank all those who contributed to this project – chiefly of course the writers themselves, whose enthusiasm carried it through amid other pressures on their busy lives. Thanks are also due to Jonathan Draper who played host for our necessary conference at Ripon College, Cuddesdon, during the preparation of the papers. Dr Robert Morgan from the University of Oxford acted as our theological consultant on that occasion and I am grateful for his critical skills and encouragement of the whole project. Thanks are also extended to my colleagues, Martin Baddeley and Phyllis Bates of the Southwark Ordination Course, for their support while this book was in preparation. Finally, I remain grateful to my wife, Christine, who has learned of the joys and frustrations of being an editor with me and deserves the greater credit in coping.

Alan Race

Pentecost 1988

Contents

Contents

The Contributors

Rex Ambler is a Quaker and lecturer in the Department of Theology at Birmingham University. He has stood as a candidate for the Green Party in local elections and also in the General Election. He is a specialist in Gandhian spirituality and is currently preparing a book on global theology.

Mark Corner teaches in the Department of Religious Studies at the University of Newcastle and has contributed articles to a number of books. His interests include the theology of liberation together with different methods of biblical interpretation, especially feminist and fundamentalist approaches.

Jonathan Draper is lecturer in systematic theology at Ripon College, Cuddesdon, and is a member of the Faculty of Theology in the University of Oxford.

Donald Evans is Professor of Philosophy in the University of Toronto, Canada. He is author of *Struggle and Fulfilment* (Collins) and the Secretary-General of the United Nations awarded him a commemorative medal for initiating observance of the International Day of Peace across Canada in 1986.

Elisabeth Holditch studied theology after a career in personnel management and specialist editing. She is a freelance writer and as a Quaker she is dedicated to the theology of peace.

Alan Race is Director of Studies for the Southwark Ordination Course. He is the author of *Christians and Religious Pluralism* (SCM Press), and editor of KOINONIA, the journal of Clergy against Nuclear Arms.

Christopher Rowland is Dean of Jesus College, Cambridge and teaches New Testament in the University. He is author of *Christian Origins* (SPCK) and *The Open Heaven* (SPCK), the latter being a study of the apocalyptic texts of Judaism and Christianity.

Contributors

Brian Russell is secretary to the Committee for Theological Education at the Advisory Council for the Church's Ministry in the Church of England.

Roger Ruston is a Dominican friar who teaches moral theology in the University of Oxford. He has written many articles on the ethics of deterrence and has served on the Catholic Bishops' Commission for International Justice and Peace. His book, *A Say in the End of the World* (Oxford University Press) is soon to be published.

Peter Selby is Anglican Bishop of Kingston. In 1988 he blessed the charcoal and ashes used in the Ash Wednesday act of protest outside the Ministry of Defence.

John MacDonald Smith is a former scientific researcher at Aldermaston Weapons Research Establishment, and a priest in the Church of England. He is Secretary of Clergy Against Nuclear Arms and is currently preparing a book on reformulating our understanding of God.

Terry Tastard is a member of the Society of St Francis. He is tutor in philosophy of religion in the University of London Extra-Mural Studies Department. He is a founder of Franciscans for Justice and Peace and works with Christian groups to develop a spirituality of social justice.

The Nuclear Horizon

Introduction

Alan Race

The dropping of the atomic bomb on Hiroshima has signalled for many people a new era in human affairs. Arthur Koestler, for example, has pointed out that since then humanity has had to live with the prospect of extinction as a species, rather than simply death as individuals.[1] Similarly, Albert Einstein's warning that 'The unleashed power of the atom has changed everything except our way of thinking,' continues to unsettle our complacency.[2] The realization that human beings now possess this capacity for self-annihilation (and for destroying much of the planet's capability to sustain life) by nuclear holocaust is a terrifying awakening.

Whether or not Koestler or Einstein are exaggerating their claims, there is no denying that the nuclear 'break' with the past has taken on symbolic meaning. Moreover, where this has proved most fertile is with the religious imagination. 'The bombing of Hiroshima was the greatest event in world history since the birth of Jesus Christ,' said the US Senator Brien 'Mr Atom' McMahon in 1952.[3] The gross distortion of this comparison would not be worth contemplating were it not for the continued capacity of Hiroshima to accrue symbolic meaning. In recent years we only need to add another example in the linkage some Christian groups, particularly in the United States, make between the Second Coming of Christ and promoting a nuclear war.

Symbolic meanings, even those surrounding nuclear catastrophe, need not always be so full of fear. The essays in this book set out to engage with the symbolic horizon of nuclear consciousness in a more positive spirit. In this they recognize that all theological work

3

is contextual. That is to say, they take seriously the insight that religious realities and theological ideas are not accidental to history but cohere with and spring from human experiences circumscribed by times and places. Since 1945 we have been living in the shadow of the nuclear threat. Yet, apart from some notable exceptions, there has been little responsible exploration of the *theological* implications of this new context.[4]

At the same time these essays recognize an ambivalence embedded in the nuclear context itself. Human beings have a profoundly vested interest in denying the nuclear threat because the potential for total destruction it represents undermines the very foundations of trust or hope in any inevitable or predictable continuing life. The invitation therefore to allow this total threat to confront us risks rejection or even derision. (It is not surprising that both reactions have been heaped on 'peace activists' in recent years). The nuclear horizon may be a stimulus for a fresh kind of theological endeavour: any resulting insight is vulnerable to the very convictions for which it stands.

This book therefore seeks a certain orientation for theology and engages in experiment, rather than follows a pre-set systematic agenda. Experiment, however, does not imply here a dispassionate stance on the part of the authors. That *God* is in the midst of the nuclear threat they have no doubt. But it is not the God who blesses the nuclear *status quo*, so much as the God who summons us out of it. Theology, the writers believe, has a definite job to do in the present circumstances to bring that out into the open. We share Gordon Kaufman's concern when he writes, 'To some of us it has become clear that a much more radical probing of the theological significance of the unprecedented new powers and responsibilities which have recently fallen to humans must be undertaken.'[5]

This is not to argue that the threat of final catastrophe is wholly new to Christian consciousness. Indeed the first-century church was resonant with such speculations, and developed its responses accordingly. However, the *nuclear* shape of our present context is new, particularly in respect of the radical responsibility that human beings now bear for the future of the planet. In the threat of nuclear annihilation the exercise of power turns against itself and responsibility for history passes into human hands. Human weakness is seen

4

to hold history to ransom. The poignancy of the present moment is that we will either learn the lesson or not. In such circumstances, theological help should be at hand.

Yet because of the ambiguity of the newness in the nuclear context, we are bound to be involved in a double movement as we engage theologically with it: we search the tradition for clues and resources which will help us to face, interpret, and confront the threatening horizon; and we submit the tradition to a new scrutiny, in the light of the new way in which we experience ourselves as human beings. These essays reflect both these emphases.

Yet even if the point about contextuality is granted, it is not immediately obvious how theologians should proceed. However, some valuable pointers have been suggested by Duncan Forrester in the collection *Ethics and Defence*, where he highlights four tasks for theology.[6] The first he calls *confessional*: though Christian theology is not prescriptive for politics, there are some policies which it cannot fail to oppose because they are in unambiguous contradiction to the Christian view of God and human flourishing. He names continuing dependence on nuclear deterrence as one such policy. The second is a *demystifying* task: like a child asking simple questions, we need to dethrone the nuclear weapon and off-set its mystique by penetrating the assumptions and disinformation surrounding it. The third task is *visionary*: it is a necessity to renew the vision of peacemaking at the heart of the Christian talk of the kingdom of God. Finally, there is the *prophetic* task: theologians might risk descending from the fence of putative neutrality and speak from an informed position on the particularities of policy. In outlining these four tasks, with considerable clarity, Forrester challenges theologians now to map out their own approaches.

From their different perspectives and with their different emphases, the writers in this book share in this four-fold outline. They would agree with Forrester when he writes:

> We should not expect theology which sees itself as a response to Jesus Christ to be always the same; but there should be an underlying complementarity and consistency in the fulfilment of the theological task.[7]

This is not to say that the essays here divide themselves neatly between Forrester's four categories, and probably that is not possible anyway. Methodologically, there are echoes of all four, overlapping within and between the different contributions. In terms of their content, they explore a number of different themes, analysing how the nuclear reality impinges on us and demands a theological response.

The agenda which is covered is not exhaustive. Yet the subjects are central to any theological reckoning with the nuclear horizon and they do follow a recognizable direction in the sections that have been created. Jonathan Draper sets the scene by examining the issue of context, and shows how there is a 'yes' and a 'no' to the priority of the nuclear threat as *the* context for all theology. It is 'yes' because in one real sense it is the whole planet which is under threat. Viewed, however, in relation to the notion of responsibility, the rich North and West ought not to dictate the theological agenda to the poor South and East where other priorities dominate. Yet the new nuclear context does require a different modelling of God from that depicted in terms of power and might if we are to recover a sense of humane values and know God as intimately bound up with our world.

Peter Selby explores further the sense in which nuclear weapons threaten humane values and perhaps even the Christian theological edifice itself – particularly any sacramental understanding of reality. He finds himself driven to reconsider the apocalyptic strand in Christian discourse for clues as to the way forward, thus throwing down a disturbing gauntlet to modern Christian interpreters and the churches. The apocalyptic theme is taken up by Christopher Rowland, who pleads for serious attention to be paid to the apocalyptic setting of the New Testament as relevant also for today. The 'abomination of desolation' (Mark 13.14) set up in the temple is an 'ultimate incarnation of wickedness', and we ought not to be shy of the risk of naming this in the threat of nuclear annihilation. In a related vein, Mark Corner unmasks the ideologically distorted interpretation of apocalyptic by the New Right Christian fundamentalist movements in the United States. He lays a choice before us between prophecy as nuclear fortune-telling and prophecy as inspiration for change after the manner of the Third World liberation theologians.

If nuclear weapons threaten humane values, then spirituality is a means for recovering them. But as we do we cannot side-step the nuclear reality itself. Rex Ambler points to the darkness of the nuclear threat as, paradoxically, the locus for human renewal in hope and trust. Only when we grasp the fact that it is human beings who are responsible for life or death *now* can we realize a different religious vision. The threat of the end is also the beginning of a spirituality which is not escapist but faithful to how life is. Concurring with this is Terry Tastard's desire to integrate our individual and corporate spiritual questing with truthfulness in public policy. Nuclear weapons are the result of a deep alienation and corruption, leaving us feeling powerless. Prayer, in the form of meditation, repentance and lament, can help us recover our integrity and freedom. The final essay in this section by Donald Evans (who contributes from the North Atlantic scene) takes these reflections a stage further by arguing for a wholistic approach to spirituality as lying at the heart of Christian peacemaking. This will involve some perhaps radical revisions in Christian understanding, but it will also deepen its incarnational essence, awaken our expanding consciousness and enable us to reduce the risk of final catastrophe.

The recovery of responsible spirituality, central in this book, would be incomplete without some consideration of the models of God which might accompany it or be implied by it. Brian Russell picks up the major point of whether and how, if human beings are now aware in the most striking manner possible of the responsibility they hold for their own individual and collective destiny, the reality of God informs the human condition. He shows how a model of God as love involves God in risk and also mutual partnership with the world, initiating 'divine promptings' as the means for luring us to life and drawing us back from the abyss. Elisabeth Holditch continues the discussion of God's compassion by setting it in the context of the wretched problem of 'permitted evil' – the task of theodicy – which after Hiroshima is posed with tortuous forceful-ness. She sees some solution in the notion of divine passibility, that God suffers with us through intimate involvement in creation, responding to its freedom, and overcoming evil with good by divine empathy. Finally, from a different perspective as a scientist, John

MacDonald Smith searches for a new model of God as a means for twinning religious values with 'science for people' as opposed to 'science for profit/exploitation'. He describes the universe as marked by self-consciously purposive evolution, which can become a model for the inseparability of God, nature and humanity. Failure to embrace the next phase of our evolution could result in species-destruction.

My own contribution stretches the models of God, and explores Christian dialogue with other religious traditions as a means of formulating a theology of peace in response to the challenge of the nuclear threat. The task before the world is enormous and it would be folly to think that Christians – or any one group – could alone bring about a major change of heart. The essay explores the nuclear threat as a focus around which theological dialogue and collaborative action might take place. Global problems, we need reminding, demand global solutions.

A further reason for assigning a central role to theology against the nuclear horizon is to place the recent ethical debate about the possession and use of nuclear weapons in a proper theological light.[8] The next section is placed purposefully therefore towards the end of the book and picks up in part on this ethical debate in the light of Christian principles. Roger Ruston follows by drawing attention to the idolatrous nature of the nuclear state and the impotence of much 'natural law' ethics to inspire the political will for change. Allowing the rules of the ethical debate to be set by those in office inevitably means capitulating to the game as played by those rules. On the other hand, worship of the true God might bring us into direct confrontation with the state. A *Postscript* continues the discussion by giving a response to the Anglican report, *Peacemaking in a Nuclear Age*.[9] The report illustrates Roger Ruston's point rather well. It is also not quite honest enough about the threat nuclear weapons themselves pose. Deterrence provides the underlying guarantee of stability.

While there is an overall complementarity in the direction the essays set for themselves, they do not pretend total unanimity. On the one hand, such differences as there are relate chiefly to the 'feel' of the newness of the nuclear context and the double movement I mentioned above (p. 5) of the theological response to it. Where a theologian places his or her emphasis in that double movement will probably depend on a mixture of motives, which may include previous training, relative judgment about the solidity of tradition in the face of cultural change, and the nature of theological language, among others. Moreover, these factors are part of any theological project today. On the other hand, there are a number of recurring themes cutting across the boundaries of particular contributions. Idolatry or the role of prophecy, for example, is not the preserve of one writer over against the others; while consideration of the radical nature of human responsibility in the face of annihilation is not far from any of them.

Yet doing theology against the nuclear horizon does recognize an urgency about our predicament. It takes its stand inevitably with those who point to the fragility of any easy short or long term accommodation with our capacity for annihilation. 'Nuclear weapons cannot be disinvented' is a truism which makes not one wit of difference to the theological task. We might just as well write 'Sin cannot be disinvented!', and pretend that faith in God is useless apart from private piety.

Theology therefore practises a certain detachment from the swings in public mood generated around arms control and political compromises. The Cold War between the power blocs of East and West may have begun to show signs of thawing in the historic INF Treaty to eliminate a whole class of nuclear weaponry (I write in the spring of 1988), and the realization that a nuclear war would yield no winners may have penetrated the minds of the political and military planners, but these factors by themselves do not signal the end of an historic and deeply entrenched antagonism between the superpowers with their allies. Western European cries for increased modernization of nuclear weapons, and the proposed Strategic Defence Initiative (Star Wars), remain signs that we are entering an even more dangerous phase in nuclear history. If we are capable of envisaging a future at all, clearly it will have to be a world-order on different terms than that which prevails at present. In one sense 'the Bomb' is but a symbol and symptom of a more wide-spread sickness.

But theology too is in the business of envisaging new futures. While it is not a prescriptive discipline for the sphere of politics and international relations, nonetheless out of its own storehouse it has contributions to make towards imagining a more wholesome way of living. This vision is only ever available provisionally. That is why for theology to make any impact, its commitment to overcoming the threat of annihilation will not be limited to blessing arms agreements and political compromises, necessary as these are as part of the process of drawing back from the abyss.

Interestingly – though perhaps not surprisingly – it is the 'peace activists' (Christians and others) who keep us alert to the changing fortunes of living under the nuclear shadow. From a position of relative insecurity and powerlessness it may be possible to 'see' the real predicament of our lives more clearly. The terms under which the nuclear debate has been conducted may be as limited as the particular perspective of those in power who set the agenda.[10] At least the vilification which the 'peace activists' have endured at the hands of the political establishment, and the marginalization suffered at the hands of the ecclesiastical establishment, could be indicators that this is the case. Those sure of their ground would not need to react so vindictively.

'Peace activists' have had to generate their own theology and they will be no strangers to some of the proposals in these essays.

No matter how one approaches the threat of nuclear extinction, there is a necessary and vital exchange which needs to press forward between theologians, the churches and 'peace activists', if theology is to make its special contribution to the new global future to which God calls us. The purpose of this book is to assist in the promotion of the serious exchange we believe is now required. It harbours the hope, perhaps audaciously, that others might follow suit, and so orientate theology towards the God whom Christians claim is on the side of life and against the nuclear horizon.

2

Theology in a Nuclear Context

Jonathan Draper

1. *The relationship between theology and its context*

It is one of the fundamental axioms of contemporary theology (and self-evident from even a cursory reading of historical theology) that there is a necessary and determinative relationship between theology and its context: there is *no* theology which is *not contextual*. One might say that a theology which carries on without paying particular and responsible attention to human reality as we encounter, experience and live it is clearly un-historical and irresponsible and would have nothing of value to offer to anyone. In any case such a theology is clearly impossible: when one tries to do a 'timeless' theology context nevertheless has its influence. The liberation, feminist and political theologians have taught us at least this much: theology not only *should be* contextual, it is so of necessity, responsive to the lived reality and experience of con-textual human beings.

Since the devastation of Hiroshima and Nagasaki, the despoila-tion of many parts of the South Pacific by nuclear weapons testing, the near-miss at Three Mile Island, the continuing problem of nuclear waste and its 'disposal', and the destruction wrought at and by Chernobyl, *one* of the great historical realities informing and shaping the context for theology today is the whole nexus of historical realities which gather around the phrase 'the nuclear question'. Importantly, it also forms a global context for theology: there is no part of our planet free from this reality (nuclear reactors and weapons apart, the presence of nomadic nuclear powered and weaponed submarines, at least, ensures this). So, a theology which proceeds without paying responsible attention to the nuclear question is clearly un-historical, irresponsible and provincial.

More than that, however, to some, like Gordon Kaufman,[1] the nuclear question puts humanity into what he claims to be a 'new historical situation', 'an unprecedented situation', a 'new religious situation'. Kaufman argues that the nuclear question puts us into a context which is not just informed, or even dominated by nuclear realities, but into one which is seen to be radically different from *any other* ever faced by humankind. Not a new dimension to reality; but an historical reality which radically alters every other historical reality and every system of meaning.

Jim Garrison, along with his informed and critical handling of the biblical material of apocalyptic, also claims that the nuclear question is *the* greatest question of our or any other age, and that because it changes everything, every other historical reality finds its meaning and place within the overarching nuclear reality, the reality of the 'plutonium culture' and the 'Age of Overkill'.[2]

Both Garrison and Kaufman argue that this new historical context also demands a new theological reality. Garrison puts it in this way:

> . . . permeating most of the Christian church is a peculiar psychic paralysis that inhibits meaningful and effective action. This paralysis, I believe, is due to the fact that the church has no *conceptual framework* within which to interpret the experience of Hiroshima and its aftermath.[3]

The claim of many who write on this subject (both religious and non-religious) is that everything is now changed. Part of the task of this essay is to explore this claim.

Because of the importance of the subject and the magnitude of the claims made by Garrison, Kaufman and others about the significance of the nuclear question, I want first to explore the relationship between theology and the nuclear context to see what that relationship is by asking the question: *Does* the nuclear reality change everything? Second I will take the answer to that question to make some suggestions as to what that implies for theology, and specifically for our understanding of God and of humanity, by asking the question: What kind of God for a Plutonium Culture? I begin, however, by making some general comments on the contextual and dialogical nature of theology, by asking the question: Who determines the theological agenda?

2. *Who determines the theological agenda?*

Old answers were being urged upon cultures and regions with new questions. People outside the North Atlantic communities felt that the older churches were not taking their questions seriously, or were trying to foist their own agenda upon them. They detected a continuing and consistent colonialism and paternalism on the part of the North Atlantic churches, which seemed to be insisting that, if they wished to be considered full-fledged Christian communities, they would have to come to think and respond like the older churches. . . . As recently as the Sixth General Assembly of the World Council of Churches at Vancouver in 1983 this was again evident: the North Atlantic churches' agenda was dominated by the question of peace and nuclear war, while the rest of the churches had to do with hunger, poverty and political repression . . . the agenda of the North Atlantic churches continued to have the upperhand in the proceedings.[4]

The question we have to face in the North Atlantic churches is this: on whose theological agenda is the nuclear question high? Is this, as Kaufman might argue, a universal item on the theological agenda, or even *the* item on the theological agenda? Even more sharply, do questions of a *potential* nuclear catastrophe even matter to the large portions of the world who face urgent *actual* questions of survival? In order even to begin to answer these questions we need to look a little more closely at the question of context in theology.

This discussion must start with the suggestion made at the beginning of this essay that all theology is contextual, done by contextual human beings.

The way in which 'context' is used in theology owes much to the word's origins in literary criticism: 'the connexion (sic) or coherence between the parts of a discourse' (*Oxford English Dictionary*). In this sense it has had an important part to play in biblical criticism, especially in discrediting (though obviously not yet eradicating) the 'proof-texting' method of exegesis. One verse, or part of a verse, means very little when the attempt to understand it is made in isolation from its wider literary context, outside its coherence or connection with the rest of the discourse or narrative of which it forms a part. In a similar way, theologians speak of 'contextual theology' or 'local theology', where theology means very little when it is unrelated, that is, not done in relation to, or done in isolation from the historical realities under which people live their lives.

Context, on the one hand, can mean the geographical 'bounda-ries' within which one lives one's life. In this (not very profound) sense my context, on a large scale, is Northern Europe; on a smaller scale, Britain; on a smaller scale yet, rural Oxfordshire. Given, however, the nature of global communications, and the growth of what has been called the 'Singapore Airport Culture', the sort of bland trans-national, even trans-'cultural' culture in which many lives are lived or by which many lives are affected, this sort of understanding of context means very little on its own.

On the other hand, the 'boundaries' within which one's life is lived can be understood more fruitfully in terms of the events and personalities which impinge on that life. In this sense Chernobyl is the context within in which much of the European landmass lives, in that the event of Chernobyl has had a profound effect on European agriculture, as well as on the area immediately surrounding the Chernobyl reactors. It is also neither accidental nor incidental that British newscasting pays particular attention to the events and personalities of Washington, DC in the USA: the nature of the 'special relationship' makes Washington a part of our context, a part of the historical realities which impinge on us and our community.

Both of these uses of 'context' lead inevitably to the proper plea of theologians such as Tissa Balasuriya for recognizing the truly 'planetary' context in which we all ultimately live.[5] In a very real sense, there is only one context, our planet: and in that context everything *is* related to everything else. What we say or do in the portion of the planet we inhabit, our part of that context, will have planetary implications and repercussions. That is, perhaps, only to restate the continual theme of the Hebrew Bible that all of world history, all of the created order and all that happens within it is the concern of Yahweh. There is nothing which stands outside the one context of Yahweh's concern for and involvement in the world. So whatever else we may want to say about context we must always recognize that *our* context cannot be isolated from the overall planetary context: in this sense, there are no 'discrete' contexts.

Having said all that, however, there is a proper sense in which we *can* talk of parts of the planetary context on their own, and describe the theological thinking arising from them as 'contextual', whatever their implications for the rest of the planetary context might be. It is entirely right that Black Christians existing under the conditions of the repressive régime of South Africa should theologize in the light of those realities; should question, for example, what kind of understanding of God they have inherited from the white ruling classes, and the kind of God their experience and their reading of the Bible leads them to understand, and so on.

An important consideration here is the relationship between contextual theologies themselves, and the relationship between a contextual theology or local church and the 'universal' church. In this connection the words of Leonardo Boff are helpful:

> The particular church is the universal church concretised . . . the particular church is the church wholly, but not the whole church. *It is the church wholly* because in each particular church is contained the whole mystery of salvation. But *it is not the whole church* because no particular church exhausts by itself the whole wealth of the mystery of salvation.[6]

Where the gospel is taken, understood and lived in a local community with all its particularities, then that community is the church wholly, but it is not the whole church. Equally, however, the 'universal' (planetary) church cannot be church at all until it is historicized or concretized in the local. The local can never be planetary; without the local the planetary can only be vacuous. Because of that, a planetary theology will always need to be a *dialògical* theology.

At its simplest, the dialogical nature of theology can be understood to be the need we have for each other. Since *no* contextual theology is the whole of theology, interdependence must characterize all theology. We need to know and respond to the needs, trouble, agony and hope of the black theologians of South Africa; we need to know the ways in which we are responsible for their agony, we need to know the ways in which we can responsibly serve them in their context. Our contexts, though different, are related.

With Boff again, we also need to recognize that the universal church is not made up of the sum of all the contextual parts, as if adding them up would give us the universal church or theology:

> The universal church is not formed of particular elements *per se*, but of elements that are common to all particular churches; by that very fact that these universal elements are particular elements. Still, what is common is not necessarily universal: the common may be the particular, found everywhere. . . . In the case of the church, the universal element is God's salvific will. . . . The particular church is the universal church (the salvific will in Christ through the Spirit) in its phenomenal, or sacramental, presentation.[7]

The question of context, then, brings us back to the theological agenda: is every context dominated by the nuclear question? Is every context dominated by it in the same way? On a planetary level, yes; every context is dominated by the nuclear question: the nuclear threat is a planetary threat. But there is also an important sense in which, while every context is dominated by the nuclear threat, not every context is dominated by it in the same way: not just because the threat is greater in some places than in others, nor just because some have suffered from nuclear realities in different ways. The question must also be considered from the perspective of differing responsibilities.

As the main creators, manufacturers, distributors, and users of nuclear weapons and technology, we in the North Atlantic and Soviet nations have a particular, a contextual, responsibility and concern for the nuclear question that non-nuclear nations do not have. We have a contextual responsibility for the nuclear question which is not the same as that of, say, the nations of the South Pacific. The nuclear question must be high on our contextual agenda in a way that reflects our particular responsibilities, as well as its general importance. We may even have to carry that responsibility for much of the rest of humanity, while theologians and others in different contexts have other historical realities higher on their agenda. We may not, for example, insist that the churches of South Korea abandon their proper claim to have human rights and the political realities of oppressive government as their agenda priority. That is the pressing historical reality under which they live. It may even be that for us to insist that others give a *potential* nuclear catastrophe a higher place on their theological and political agenda than the *actual* suffering of the politically oppressed or the starving millions, is simply an attempt to avoid the hard questions of reality. It may even be another form of patronizing paternalism to insist that *we* in the North Atlantic churches know what is most important. The context, in this sense, sets the theological agenda.

From the perspective of our talk about God, this whole discussion could have begun with the notion that it is God who sets the theological agenda. If, as we preach and believe, the initiative in theology rests with God, then the theological agenda must be set by God. It is to God that we respond; it is our relationship to God that we explore in theology. No matter the agenda of the world, our agenda as Christians is God's agenda.

Of course our theological agenda must be in response to God's initiative: but how do we determine what God is 'up to'? If we are to take an incarnational theology seriously, and if we are to take equally seriously the involvement of God in every aspect of God's creation, then we must look for God and respond to God where we are, in our context. We must learn to see God, to know God in the very stuff of which our existence is made. The theological agenda, like the rest of God's mission in the world, does not drop out of the sky, like the agenda for a church committee dropping out of the post. The agenda is there, God is there waiting for us to see and respond.

3. *Does the nuclear reality change everything?*

To answer the question of who sets the theological agenda by stating that the context does, is not yet to answer the question of whether or not it should be at the top of *every* theological agenda. Does the nuclear reality change everything? If so, what does it change, and how does it change it?

17

As mentioned above, to many theologians (Kaufman, Garrison and others) the nuclear reality *has* changed everything. Kaufman puts it like this:

> The stark fact of total human responsibility for the earthly future of humanity, which a potential nuclear catastrophe symbolises, calls into question all . . . traditional talk – held together so tightly and meaningfully in the symbol of the divine sovereignty – of God's power and purposes and love as the proper and only adequate ground for hope in our desperate situation. This fact demands that we ask much more seriously than many have yet done whether it is not necessary to reconsider some of the most fundamental axioms of western religious symbolism and faith. Humanity's 'coming of age', to use Bonhoeffer's phrase, means that traditional images of divine providential care guaranteeing ultimate human fulfilment have become not only outmoded; they have become misleading and dangerous in certain important respects, and they must be thoroughly reworked.[8]

Clearly, Kaufman is on to something very important here when he speaks of what the potential nuclear catastrophe *symbolizes*, of our *religious symbolism*, and of a need to rework our images of God and God's providential care. Kaufman is urging us to take a closer and deeper look into what might be called the 'semiotics of Hiroshima': in what ways (if any) do our signs and symbols, images and metaphors correspond to or, to use the more helpful phrase of Janet Martin Soskice, 'depict' reality?[9] If nothing else, the nuclear question has forced us to look more closely at ourselves, and in so doing, to alter our perceptions of the world in which we live and our part in it. In that sense, if no other, the nuclear question has changed much.

Earlier in this essay I noted our human dependence on the creation for our understanding of ourselves, of who we are in relation to our creator. Our experience of the world and of ourselves in the world and in relation to other 'selves', shapes our self-understanding. Taking that a stage further, there are important senses in which we are also dependent on the creation and the self-understanding it gives us, for understanding our creator; or perhaps better, we are dependent on the creation for our ability to articulate our perceptions of God. We do not know God apart from God's creation; we do not know ourselves apart from God's creation.

This is perhaps something of the truth that Luther articulated in his demand for theology to be a *theologia crucis*; of understanding revelation as 'revelation under a contrary'. The epistemological point is important: all our knowledge of God is mediated knowledge, knowledge in a context: there is no *theologia gloriae* apart from the *theologia crucis*. If the nuclear context has brought about a change in our perceptions of ourselves, then it will not be surprising to find that it brings about changes in our perceptions of God.

If, then, our knowledge of ourselves and our knowledge of God is always knowledge in a context, what kind of knowledge or perception of ourselves can be found in seeing Hiroshima and Chernobyl as symbols? On the one hand, they can be seen to be symbols of the staggering creative potential and ability of human beings. To be able to harness such vast and unimaginably powerful forces is an achievement of no small magnitude, and stands witness both to human ability and human self-assurance. We can accomplish much to which we put our minds. On the other hand, they stand as symbols of the enormity of human folly, the height of human arrogance and self-centredness, the depths, the destructive depths, even, of human sin. These can be seen to stand as symbols of our greatness *and* of our depravity; of our wisdom *and* of our folly; of our high potential for good *and* of our high potential for evil.

Hiroshima and Chernobyl are not the only symbols which might express these truths, and they need not be learned only here. No more eloquent a symbol of human depravity is needed than that of the Jewish Holocaust; no more striking symbol of our potential for good and our potential for evil than grain mountains and mass starvation. The knowledge of ourselves arising from the historical realities which are our context paint a picture of human extremes to which the nuclear symbols add only reinforcement.

However, the recent knowledge we have of the *limits* of our potential, that we can now accomplish our own destruction in a complete way, brings us hard up against another realization. What previously we could only do on a limited scale, that is, destroy a people or an environment, we now realize we can do on a global scale. The truly global nature of our capabilities is new. But this itself is only paradoxical: it is an extension by degree of what has always been within our grasp – the destruction of ourselves and others and our environment. In this sense, the nuclear question has not changed anything: we have always been free to be self-destructive. We have always been subject to our own hubris: only now we can see its potential and perhaps its final expression.

But does this change what we perceive about God and how we express those perceptions? The call of God to humanity remains the same: 'build with me a humanity worthy of the name "the people of God".' While we may no longer wish to articulate that call in, say, the language of Greek metaphysics, the call remains. The *pattern* of Christian perception of God also remains: it is in the cross that we perceive our God most clearly. It is in the darkness that we begin to see the light; it is in death that life is born; it is in humanity that we see God. Insofar as we see in ourselves the potential for both creation and destruction (to a degree, now, never before imagined), so we can perceive something of God, so we can perceive something of the staggering nature of radical human evil. A nuclear context sharpens the focus for all of us.

There is a further consideration here. If we are to write, and more importantly live, a truly contextual theology, then the nuclear realities, in all their inter-related complexity with other historical realities, must, by the very nature of their urgency, be taken absolutely seriously in our theologizing. It may mean that for us they must assume a priority over other 'items' on the theological agenda. If the way in which we know ourselves is within a nuclear context, then it is also in that context that we must work out our salvation and articulate our perceptions of God. If we can no longer express our understanding of the human condition through, say, an Augustinian doctrine of original sin, then we must do it through the symbols of the Holocaust and Hiroshima. If it will no longer do to express our understanding of God through the language and symbols of a past age or philosophical world-view, then we must do so through these contemporary symbols. Any understanding of incarnation demands at least that much.

4. *What kind of God for a plutonium culture?*

It should not be a matter for regret that some of our traditional images of God might have to go. Images of God as all powerful, the Lord mighty in battle, and so on have often (some would say, only) led humanity to the brink of self-destruction by the way we have modelled ourselves on that image of God. It may be, further, that these traditional images of God never really did an adequate job of depicting the reality we call God in any case. Has God been known only in human military or monarchical contexts for all these years? Or is there a whole hidden 'side' of God that has been, if not repressed, then obscured, only revealed now that we have begun to pay some attention to the marginalized of our world? What kind of images emerge from these different contexts? How might they serve to move us away from self-destruction and towards genuine human community?

We have seen that one of the great historical realities under which we live, even a dominating one, are the nuclear realities and the potential for extinction that they carry. Through that context we have learned that we are immensely powerful and that we have a genuine capacity for destruction of which our forbears never conceived. We have also learned from the Holocaust, Hiroshima and Chernobyl that the God in whom we believe is not a God who will prevent disaster unaided. God will not prevent us from doing that of which we are able. We stand in need of new metaphors to help us in depicting this new perception of reality: the reality of ourselves, our world and our God.

Kaufman and Garrison, and others, such as Sallie McFague and Jürgen Moltmann[10] all argue in their different ways that we need an ecologically responsible understanding of ourselves, our world and God. They also argue that images and models of ourselves and God that portray humanity as entirely dependent on God for its self-preservation no longer depict reality in any meaningful way. Moltmann tries to rehabilitate more conventional images, as does Garrison, trying to breathe a new reality into old images. Kaufman and McFague make the more radical attempt at going beyond them to explore new images and models which might bring along with them a proper sense of our co-responsibility with God. I would like

21

to follow the method of Moltmann and Garrison to try to achieve something of what Kaufman and McFague are attempting. Part of the reason for this attempt lies in the important truth that new understandings and symbols for God do not, indeed cannot, arise in a vacuum: that would only lead to unintelligibility. New symbols and images must always *emerge* out of, from, or in relation to a tradition. Traditions and symbols may, even must be transformed, and new symbols may emerge (Hiroshima, as a multi-faceted symbol has done so), but we may not simply create new ones.

5. *Exodus and the co-operative God*

Taking the natural movement of what we have seen in this essay so far, I want to approach this final part from a slightly different, but complementary angle, and end by suggesting some guidelines for the way in which our understanding of God might be developed and expressed. As a way into discovering some of those guidelines, I want to draw out a few ideas from the story of the Exodus of the Israelites from Egypt. I do this for two reasons: (1) In Christian theology, an important part of the tradition out of which, from which, and in relation to which arises an articulation of the Christian faith is the Bible. (2) The Exodus story is paradigmatic not only for Jewish self-understanding, but also, for much of contemporary theology. In that sense it forms part of a wider contemporary theological tradition within which much current thought about God is done.

If we take this fundamental paradigm of Jewish self-understanding – the Exodus – and begin a fresh exegesis of it to bring out some of the salient points again, we may find that the tradition is capable of bearing the weight of our new context. To do this, however, we must also be prepared along the way to abandon some of the understand-ings of the Exodus found in the tradition in order to use the insights which can be drawn from it. This should not be problematic, as we must join with Jews in all ages in rejecting all 'absolute' images of God, no matter how cherished they might be, because all images, if absolutized, are idolatrous.

In broad strokes, the Exodus story speaks of the movement of a people out of oppression and slavery into a new situation of freedom and control over their own destiny. One of the key elements in that story is the striking way in which God and humanity co-operate in the whole enterprise. God 'purposes' to bring the people out of Egypt, but tells Moses that he (Moses) is to lead the people in this strike for freedom.

> The Lord said, 'I have indeed seen the misery of my people in Egypt. I have heard them crying out because of their slave drivers, and I am concerned about their suffering. So I have come down to rescue them . . . So now, *go. I am sending you* to Pharaoh to bring my people the Israelites out of Egypt.' (Ex. 3.7ff.)

Along the way, in the desert wanderings, the people are enjoined to co-operate, to be and become a people of God; when they arrive in the promised land it becomes the calling of the people to get on with the business of creating a godly human community. In all of this the Israelites are discovered by and discover God in this struggle, in all of the difficulties of forging human community which is also godly community. Even the law, central as it is to Jewish self-understanding, is given not so much to prove that God is a law-giver, but to demonstrate that human beings and the conditions under which they live are central to understanding the concerns of God. In all of this, there is no sense in which the people of God are 'dependent' on God for everything, or that God will fight their (literal or metaphorical) battles for them: they co-operate with God for everything. A constant refrain of the prophets is for Israel to remain faithful to their calling to be a godly human community, and to forsake all that detracts from or inhibits that.

The accomplishment of God's 'purpose' depends on God's people; that was so then and is so now. The whole of the Hebrew Bible and the history of the church is the story of people in co-operative movement with God; striving with God to create godly human community. The people of God (indeed all of humanity) always have genuine responsibility, always have a 'veto' in what God purposes simply by exercising their freedom to do what they will. God's 'purposes' are not so much frustrated by this as they are denied, not done, left unaccomplished. (Though an important part of what the people of God learn throughout their history is that there are others, outside the immediate family of faith, who join with God in God's mission in the world. Whoever strives for godly human community is partner with God). God remains powerless in the face of the non-co-operation of humanity. 'God has no hands on earth but ours'. . . . This expresses the beginning of a theological anthropology and a theology of mission.

We must then strip away the triumphalist, patriarchal and hierarchical imagery surrounding this co-operative God of the tradition, and seek to 'clothe' that God in images that speak of that co-operative reality. God should no longer be viewed as being like a king, nor like a military strong-man, nor like the male head of a clan or family with absolute authority. These are images and models that have grown to stand in the way of understanding God, that have allowed Christians to avoid their real and urgent responsibilities in this world. More than at any time in our history, with the new knowledge we have of ourselves through the nuclear context, this can no longer serve our worship, our ethics or our piety. To proclaim the God of patriarchy, hierarchy and guaranteed triumph has become to proclaim an idol and a blasphemy.

The philosophical groundwork for a more co-operative model for God has been admirably laid in Grace Jantzen's book *God's World, God's Body*,[11] where God is understood as inextricably bound to God's creation and where the future of God is bound up with the future of our world. Moltmann, too, seeks to understand God as being in essential and interdependent relationship with God's creation, arguing that mechanistic or Cartesian views of the world and of God, which see an unbridgeable gulf between God and the world, as having had disastrous consequences historically, and potentially catastrophic consequences in a nuclear present and future. He writes,

> In God there is no one-sided relationship of superiority and subordination, command and obedience, master and servant, as Karl Barth maintained in his theological doctrine of sovereignty, making this the starting point for his account of all analogously antithetical relationships: God and the world; heaven and earth; soul and body; and, not least, man and woman too. In the triune God is the mutuality and the reciprocity of love.
>
> Our starting point here is that all relationships which are

analogous to God reflect the primal, reciprocal indwelling and mutual interpenetration of the trinitarian perichoresis: God *in* the world and the world *in* God. . . . There is no such thing as solitary life. . . . All living things – each in its own specific way – live in one another and with one another, from one another and for one another.[12]

The models of God which our Plutonium Culture needs, which will also serve our cultures of mass starvation, genocide, oppression and greed, should therefore reflect this essential inter-relatedness of God and the world, of ourselves and each other. Our models of God, therefore, will need to be exploratory rather than definitive, relative rather than absolute, symbiotic rather than hierarchical, about collaboration rather than sovereignty. Any model we use for God must take seriously the nature of reality as we experience and try to express it. As we grow in our awareness of the essentially symbiotic nature of created reality, so too we must explore images and models of God that reflect that reality.

These are the only kinds of models that can adequately depict the kind of reality we know to be important in our world and for ourselves. Without those sorts of models and images, God is nothing more than a hindrance to our grappling with reality. The God of power and might, if that God ever truly existed, is now dead and must be buried. Our knowledge of ourselves and the reality of our world demands no less.

Continuing Apocalyptic

3

Apocalyptic – Christian and Nuclear[1]

Peter Selby

'When the sabbath was over Mary Magdalene and Mary the mother of James and Salome bought spices so that they might go and anoint Jesus, and very early on the first day of the week they went to the tomb when the sun had risen and they were saying to one another, "Who will roll away the stone for us from the door of the tomb"; and looking up they saw that the stone was rolled back, for it was very large; and entering the tomb they saw a young man sitting on the right side, dressed in a white robe, and they were amazed. And he said to them, "Do not be amazed. You seek Jesus of Nazareth who was crucified. He has risen. He is not here; see the place where they laid him. But go tell his disciples and Peter that he is going before you to Galilee; there you will see him as he told you." And they went out and fled from the tomb, for trembling and astonishment had come upon them and they said nothing to anyone for they were afraid' (Mark 16.1–8).

Precisely at 8.15.17 a.m. the bomb-bay doors of the Enola Gay snapped open. The plane lurched upwards nearly ten feet, suddenly 9,000 pounds lighter. Inside the bomb a timer tripped the first switch in the firing circuit, letting the electricity travel a measured distance towards the detonator. At 5,000 feet above the ground a barometric switch was triggered. At 1,890 feet the detonator was activated, the bomb exploding at 8.16, forty-three seconds after falling from the Enola Gay.

In the first milli-second after detonation, a pin-prick of purplish-red light expanded into a flowing fireball half a mile in diameter; the temperature at its core was 50,000,000 degrees

Fahrenheit. At Ground Zero, some two thousand feet directly underneath the explosion, temperatures reached several thousand degrees, melting the surface of granite 1,000 yards away. Nine hundred yards from the epicentre, several thousand soldiers, including one American prisoner of war, were doing their morning exercises in the courtyard of Hiroshima Castle: they were instantly incinerated, their charred bodies burnt into the ground.

Watching from below, one child remembered later the entire sequence leading up to this first milli-second:

> I was watching the aeroplane the whole time . . . Suddenly a thing like a white parachute came falling. Five or six seconds later everything turned yellow in one instant. It felt the way it does when you get the sunlight straight into your eye . . .

To those aboard the Enola Gay, observing the scene at an altitude of 29,000 feet eleven miles away, the scene was quite spectacular, as the tailgunner, Sergeant George Caron, recalls:

> A column of smoke rising fast. It has a fiery red core, a bubbling mass purple-grey in colour, with that red core . . . It's all turbulent. Fires are springing up everywhere, like flames shooting out of a huge bed of coals . . . Here it comes, the mushroom shape . . . like a mass of bubbling molasses . . . It's very black, but there is a purplish tint to the cloud. The base of the mushroom looks like a heavy undercast that is shot through with flames. The city must be below that . . .

It was, Caron remembered later, like a 'peep into hell'.

So complete was the destruction that a history professor recalls that:

> I climbed Hijiyama Hill and looked down. I saw that Hiroshima had disappeared . . . I was shocked by the sight . . . What I felt then and feel now I just can't explain with words. Of course I saw many dreadful scenes after that – but that experience, looking down and finding nothing left of Hiroshima – was so shocking that I simply can't express what I felt. I could see Koi (a suburb at the opposite end of the city) and a few buildings standing . . . But

Hiroshima didn't exist – that was mainly what I saw – Hiroshima just didn't exist.

'Such a weapon', he was to recall later, 'has the power to make everything into nothing'.[2]

Theology has from the beginning begun with event, with narrative: and that rather flat narrative of Hiroshima is, and has to remain, the context of this essay, except only that the scale of the destruction which we are now contemplating is, of course, vastly greater than is described in that narrative.

The interesting thing is to know what possible contribution theology, as we have known it, could make to the contemplation of that narrative. In the report *The Church and the Bomb* there isn't actually a great deal of theology. The report does say some very straightforwardly uncontroversial theological things, but its main concerns are with strategy, with weapons, with facts and with politics, and that's quite right because that's what this issue is, in the end, about. But let me quote one theological paragraph:

> The Old Testament is clear that creation is an action of God and not of humankind and that its ultimate purposes and aims are beyond human understanding. The trusteeship which men and women exercise over creation enables them to participate in God's plan. This is what human freedom is for and it carries immense responsiblities. It is a freedom which can be used for good or evil. These fundamental biblical insights into the human responsibility towards creation, and the consequent obligation to work out the meaning of faith in relation to the world and its concerns, have a poignant relevance for our times in the light of the virtually incalculable destructive power of nuclear weapons.[3]

And it is that poignant relevance which the report does not particularly set out to explore but which I would like to explore briefly here.

For the 'poignant relevance' lies in the questions which nuclear weapons ask about whether human responsibility has passed beyond the point that we are able to bear; and secondly what kind of a God, if there be such, could possibly allow things to reach such a pass that human responsibility extends to the point where it could bring about the ending of human history. The struggle that is expressed in Jonathan Schell's book *The Fate of the Earth*[4] is a struggle with the question of extinction. He makes the point that there is a very important distinction between death on the one hand, even in massive quantities, and extinction on the other. What we are contemplating in the case of nuclear weapons is actually the possibility of extinction. And extinction differs from death, says Schell, in that while death is the end of life, extinction is the end of birth. Nuclear weapons remind us that human beings are not only mortal they are also natal; they have to have a beginning as well as, it is certain, they have an end. It is this apocalyptic aspect of the nuclear situation which connects it with the resurrection narrative with which this essay began. It seems that it is apocalypse that we are indeed into: and it is my intention here to contemplate some of the implications of the fact that the Christian tradition does contemplate apocalypse, and the relevance of that for our consideration of nuclear weapons. As I read the narrative of the Hiroshima event in Garrison's book I couldn't help remembering the occasion when Christopher Evans addressed a conference on 'The Resurrection', and was endeavouring to explain apocalyptic and eschatalogical language. I remember his saying:

> It's no use asking (in relation to the thought-forms of apocalyptic) what happens *after* the resurrection, because resurrection is not a what-happens-after-it kind of thing.

It seems to me that nuclear weapons are in a sense also, at least in their potential, not a what-happens-after-them kind of thing. And Schell is right to draw to our attention that what we are contemplating is that we have arrived at the point where extinction is a real possibility.

Now the possibility of extinction, the possibility of the end of human existence, also puts us in communication with those of our forbears who brought the first five books of the Bible into existence, because they too were aware, as primitive people have to be aware, of the fragility of ordinary human existence. And they expressed that fragility by handing on myths, by telling stories about how there was a time when the world was not, and by speaking of an 'event' which brought out of a watery chaos the history that we know as our life But the fragility of that life was something which they also continued to be aware of and to describe by their use of a myth which is common to most ancient peoples, the myth of the deluge.[5] And the myth of the deluge is remarkable in our tradition for the way it ends; you will recall that the deluge happens, in our tradition, because of the anger of a righteous God at what human beings have made of the creation of their freedom within a bounded, created order.

The deluge arises from the divine anger; but of course it is no solution, because at the end of the deluge God has still to make a decision whether to retain any commitment to those creatures who had made such a mess of things before. That policy-decision, that divine policy-decision, is expressed clearly and graphically at the end of the deluge story in Genesis 8 in the form of something God says to Godself:

> Yahweh said in his heart, 'I will never again curse the ground because of humans beings for the imagination of the human heart is evil from their youth, neither will I ever again destroy every living creature as I have done, while the earth remains seed time and harvest cold and heat, summer and winter, day and night shall not cease' (Gen. 8.21–22).

Thus human history was understood to be lived within a secure and bounded realm, a realm bounded by a beginning and later understood to be bounded by an end. And the relevance of the resurrection story that I quoted is that the resurrection story also is an account of the way in which that fragility is once again confirmed and affirmed in the discovery that within the human realm, within the historic realm, all the hoped-for fulfilment of God's purpose had been revealed in Jesus crucified.

Now it seems that we are confronted in our age with the situation that the fragile guarantee within which human life is lived has been taken out of God's hands. No longer do we live in a situation in which we are given freedom to live lives of justice and hope and peace, within a bounded realm, the security of which is somehow out of our hands. We are now in the position where the very bounded security, which has been the precondition of purposive human existence, *is itself in our hands and is itself under threat*. That

33

seems to be the dramatic significance of the fact that we are faced with the possibility of real extinction. And that is a transmutation of what had been the basis of our ethical thinking, and of every other kind of human thinking, as Schell observes in his book. For all human ethical thinking, all political thinking, and all human planning has been based on the notion that there was at any rate some security to the universe of discourse. Yet it is precisely the universe of discourse, and not only of discourse, that is itself under threat.

This kind of thinking is not the result of my selecting in an arbitrary way the story of the covenant with Noah as the paradigm of the Christian understanding of the safety of history. There are other doctrinal elements within the Christian tradition which also are faced with a fundamental threat as a result of the creation of nuclear weapons. There is, for example, the whole tradition of sacramentality, the notion that material things are capable of mediating ultimate reality to us. That sacramentality is represented by certain key elements, the water of baptism and the bread and wine of the eucharist chiefly, and is in principle available to the entire material universe.

There are two sides to a sacramental tradition. The first is the one I have already mentioned, namely that the sacraments mean that the material world mediates that which is beyond itself and which gives material life its significance – in the Anglican formularies the outward and visible sign of inward and spiritual grace. That is the positive side. But the negative side is that Christians therefore speak of a God who has bound up his fate with materiality in a quite fundamental sense. It is not simply that a bonus has been conferred on material things, that they can do what materialists don't realize they can: it is also that they are somehow billed as the essential constituents and ingredients of the divine activity towards the world.

Now we are faced in the existence of nuclear weapons with a threat to sacramentality of a quite unprecedented kind, for we are now capable of causing an irrevocable mutation to the structure of being, such that the present structure of being as we have known it could not be recreated. And that threatens not simply our material existence, but it threatens also the basic manner of our material, sacramental apprehension of the divine. And fundamental to the threat of possible extinction is a threat to all human and personal values; for value depends upon the existence of sentient and valuing beings such as we understand human beings to be.

The ending of the human species therefore is actually the ending of value, and if I may come to the extremity of my unorthodoxy, before returning to what might look more mainline, it seems to place fundamentally under threat any Christian understanding of revelation. For however much it may be orthodox to maintain that the existence of God does not depend upon a human society to apprehend God, it seems that in actual fact the entire manner of the divine self-disclosure to, and relationship with, the universe is placed in jeopardy the moment you consider that it is possible, and might be legitimate, and might even be necessary, to bring the entire universe as we have known it, to an end. So what I am suggesting is that nuclear weapons place under threat most of the theological edifice to which we have grown accustomed.

So we are faced with apocalypse; and like the first observers of the crucifixion and the resurrection of Jesus we are faced with something which we have not been led to suppose, namely apocalypse entering into the possibilities of human history. But unlike the apprehension of the meaning of the crucifixion and resurrection of Jesus, our apprehension of nuclear weapons is not felt to be life-giving but only potentially death-dealing. Those who have thought about the ethics of nuclear weapons, and those who are campaigning for the banning of the bomb, have already drawn attention many times to the fact that death from a nuclear holocaust is not something in the future, nor is it something in the past. It is not confined to the reality and aftermath of Hiroshima and Nagasaki nor is it something that we only fear and dread for our future. The possibilities of nuclear holocaust are present with us in the result to millions of people on this planet of the diversion into the arms-race of resources which would otherwise be available for the feeding of the hungry and caring for the sick. We are thus already in the process of killing people, though we are not at the moment in the process of bringing about extinction.

But the presence of the possibility of extinction is having a present theological effect in relation to our entire value system and our entire religious perception. For, far more than we realize, our institutions and the things which we find most valuable in living are related to the possibility of a future. We have always had, of course, to wrestle with mortality; people get married till death them do part, and people create societies knowing that their children and not they will benefit or suffer from what they create. Human beings have always had to wrestle therefore with their own death; but I don't believe it has been the case before that people have had to wrestle with their *natality*, that is to say with the fact that future generations require an environment in which they can be born, and that that environment is no longer assured.

We are faced paradoxically with a situation in which the more violently we protest our right to create larger and larger stores of nuclear weapons, the more violently do we at the same time protest the value of those former values, those firm social political and religious values which nuclear weapons place most under threat. Jonathan Schell makes some important links between military expansion and the conservative instinct.

It is fully understandable that in the face of the distortion and disintegration of human relationships in a doom-ridden world, a conservative longing for a richer more stable and more satisfying social existence should spring up. Unfortunately however this longing, instead of inspiring us to take political measures that would remove the world from jeopardy and thus put life on a solid footing again, all too often takes the form of a simple wish that the world would stop being the way it is now and return to its former state with what are often called old values intact. Rather than take cognizance of the radical causes of the world's decline, with a view to doing something about them, these would-be upholders of the past tend to deny the existence of our new situation. It is only one more part of this denial, the most dangerous part, to imagine that war too still exists in its traditional form in which one's enemies can be defeated in the field of battle without bringing an end to everything. Conservatism in personal and social questions has often gone together with militarism in the past but now the combination is far more perilous than ever before; it represents a denial of what the world has now become which could lead to the end of the world. If a nation indulges itself in the illusion that even with nuclear arms, war is possible, and that victory can be won with them, it risks bringing about its own and the world's extinction by mistake. Alert and realist conservatives by contrast would see that everything that anyone might wish to conserve is threatened by nuclear weapons and would recognize in them a threat, not only to the old values, but to any values whatever, and instead of dreaming of the vanished cause of past times they would place themselves in the forefront of a movement for disarmament.[6]

Schell says that all our institutions of personal value are compromised by the threat of extinction. Marriages are contracted in the face of the possible non-existence of a future. And while it may be true that an individual marriage can exist in perfect integrity with no intention to bring children into the world, marriage in general is surely predicated on the assumption that human being and human society is worth giving a future. Political institutions likewise are predicated on the notion that our children have some expectations of us and have a right to those expectations.

All those expectations are compromised in a situation in which we seriously entertain the possibility of rupturing the boundary that surrounds our life, the space that exists within which human history is available for us to live out. The covenant with Noah has been placed irrevocably now into our hands and we have actually to find some way of recognizing – this recognition is of course a political matter – that each and every human institution of any value is being corrupted in the present, is being extinguished here and now by the compromising contradiction of our willingness to defend it by the weapons of extinction.

Who will actually apprehend the fundamental theological crisis that nuclear weapons place us in? I cannot help making some interior connections between that narrative of the women at the tomb and recent developments in the anti-nuclear campaign, developments that are public and well-known like the Greenham Common demonstration. I suspect that we have reached the ultimate symbol, not only of our capacity to plan and create a technological world, but of certain assumptions under which we have laboured in running that world. It may be that the apprehension of the true significance of where we have arrived will have to lie with those people who were disinherited from that former world anyway; that I don't know. But I do know that the current crisis about nuclear weapons has reactivated for me the apocalyptic strand in the Christian tradition, and has made me ask the question what steps can be taken to secure the boundaries of our existence and the sacramentality of the material world in which our existence is lived out. And in looking at that, I have wondered what steps religious people in particular need to be taking to see how we can apprehend in the horror of that Hiroshima narrative what it seemed to be given to some people to apprehend in the Good Friday events, namely the challenge of moving from the actuality of death, to the possibility at any rate of life.

4

Discerning the 'Abomination of Desolation'

Christopher Rowland

Ten years ago I remember receiving a postcard from a North American friend. In cartoon form it depicted a terrible scene of destruction in a poor modern parody of a Bosch painting. Aeroplanes were crashing into towerblocks and cars careering, driverless and out of control along motorways. The scene was one of destruction and chaos. It depicted the situation, post-rapture, after Jesus had come to draw the elect to himself leaving behind those destined to destruction in a world of chaos. Here was the fulfilment of the words in the gospels:

> I tell you in that night there will be two men in a bed; one will be taken and another left. There will be two women grinding together; one will be taken and the other left (Luke 17.34).

I showed the card to one of my students who told the story of her childhood before she had been converted when she had been taught by her parents that she might be one of those left behind. She recalled nights of horror and sorrow wondering whether she might be left an orphan in a world bereft of the elect and God.

Those stories are a potent reminder that apocalyptic and eschatological imagery is part of our contemporary culture. It is tempting to distance ourselves from such extravagances, not least because the apocalyptic tradition has a reputation for disturbing, and indeed fragmenting, the fabric of religion down the centuries. But for those of us whose task it is to interpret the canon of scripture

39

that would seem to be an abrogation of our responsibility. We may like to think that a mark of our respectability in academe has been important for theology as it has sought to justify its place in a secular university. Nevertheless we ignore the power of the apocalyptic tradition both at our peril and to our religious and imaginative impoverishment, particularly in a political climate which is inimical to the basic tenets of the Judaeo-Christian tradition. Our so-called critical 'objectivity' may in effect be a way of putting distance between ourselves and the struggles of our contemporary world in which religions and their various scriptures are having their part to play. In this situation it is no longer easy to pretend that we can opt out, because the scholarly rules of interpretation are not being followed. A question must be raised as to the justification of our aloofness from the struggles which are going on in our world. The quest for objectivity and appropriate use of the text are in themselves no barrier to involvement in those struggles. It is precisely *in the midst* of those struggles that a critical reflection on our reading emerges, not in the mistaken belief that the seclusion of the ivory-tower can best give us that objectivity which will correct the distortions of the committed reading. We need to be clear about our own prejudices concerning the apocalyptic and eschatological tradition. Some may involve us in a necessary suspicion of some contemporary interpretation, but others will arise from the consensus-oriented quest for stability which may have been appropriate for an age when there was common ground on basic issues of peace and justice but seem singularly inappropriate now.

Today the book of Revelation can be the resource of both ends of the political spectrum. On the one hand, it has been a poem of hope to oppressed Christians throughout the ages. On the other hand, it offers a dream of miraculous rescue at the rapture of the saints which serves as a licence for escape from political struggle. The panoramas of destruction with no human solution offered but the flight from the world, are helping to create the conditions through which they become scenes from a self-fulfilling prophecy. This is so because some of the most powerful men in the world see in them a picture of the world hurtling to disaster from which they can be rescued in the nick of time by the return of the Christ to save the born-again Christians from the nuclear holocaust. Our age is one which has shown itself attracted to apocalyptic symbolism. Moreover, it is a fascination which has come to the fore at different periods in the life of the church (e.g. with Joachim of Fiore at the end of the twelfth century), and so it runs like a thread through history, linking our own day with the age of Jesus.

That was a period of foreboding and uncertainty in which a fragile peace in Roman Judaea was finally swept away in a violent and bloody revolt which led to the decimation of Judaism as Jesus of Nazareth would have known it. In AD 70 the magnificent Temple in Jerusalem was destroyed and with it the sacrificial system and the *raison d'être* for thousands of priests. It was a terrible event the reason for which lay in the history of the period and the frustrated hopes of a nation which in the end allowed the possibility of the fulfilment of hope to triumph over the reality of military power. Unless we recognize the character of the age in which he lived we shall not fully understand the challenge of Jesus who earnestly demanded of his contemporaries that they understand the signs of the times.

The Jewish historian Josephus has left us snippets of information about various figures and movements whose leaders claimed to be called by God to be agents of liberation into a new era of prosperity for the people of God.

> . . . the wretched people were deluded at that time by charlatans and those who claimed to be messengers from God. They did not give heed to, nor believe, the manifest portents that foretold the coming desolation of Jerusalem, but as if completely thunderstruck and bereft of all rational thought they disregarded the plain warnings of God. In adversity human beings are quickly persuaded; but when the deceiver actually pictures liberation from the horrors of the present, then those who are undergoing suffering often completely abandon themselves to such expectation . . . (Josephus, *Jewish War* vi. 285, Loeb edition).

In the light of first-century Jewish history the story of Jesus of Nazareth is just one more account of the tragic failure of the pursuit of the millennium and the dashing of raised hopes. Perhaps Jesus of Nazareth appeared in exactly this light to those who viewed with increasing apprehension the turmoil of first-century Galilee and Judaea.

Jesus of Nazareth was not the only Jesus to proclaim a message of doom. We have the story of another Jesus whose prophetic protest was also greeted with persecution and derision:

> One Jesus, son of Ananias . . . suddenly began to cry, A voice from the east, a voice from the west, a voice from the four winds; a voice against Jerusalem and against the sanctuary . . . The magistrates supposing . . . that the man was under some super-natural impulse, brought him before the Roman governor; there, although flayed to the bone with sources, he neither sued for mercy nor shed a tear but merely introducing the most mournful of variations into his ejaculation, responded to each stroke with 'Woe to Jerusalem' (Josephus, *Jewish War* vi. 300f.).

What difference, if any can we detect between this Jesus and the other Jesus? The major difference lies in the conviction of Jesus of Nazareth that the manifestation of God's sovereignty in the affairs of men and women would be in the present age, not in some otherworldly future or solely in the far distant past of Exodus and entry into the Promised Land. The presence of God in human history was to be seen in present actions; God was not far off enthroned above the heavens: 'the kingdom of God is in your midst'. The presentation of Jesus' life in the first three gospels furnishes ample evidence that Jesus thought that the critical moment in history had come: 'the time (*kairos*) has come to fruition; the reign of God has drawn near repent and believe in the good news'. Immediately preceding those words in Mark's gospel Jesus comes to be baptized by John. The account of that baptism resembles the prophetic call visions of the Old Testament and has all the appearances of a prophetic commission. He believed himself inspired by the spirit which once inspired the prophets, whose return would herald the new age of the fulfilment of God's purposes for creation. The cry of the prophet who regarded the rending of the heavens a prelude to the eschatological salvation is fulfilled as the Spirit of God rends the heavens and anoints the one who proclaims the imminence of the reign of God.

The gospel narrates the actions of Jesus in healings and in expelling the impure spirits: signs that the strong man is being bound and the powers of darkness overcome. The existing order is challenged, and Jesus' actions and words are deeply offensive to many of the religious and political authorities, for he offers hope and healing to those on the margins of society. Jesus' message of the kingdom of God was about a new order in which the powers of darkness were to be (and were already being) overthrown: 'If I by the finger of God cast out demons, then you know that kingdom of God has come upon you.' Jesus was not just a visionary who could report that he had seen Satan fall like lightning from heaven. He was struggling against the forces of evil, in the dislocation of individuals, who embody the fragmentation of a divided community.

Those stories of the confrontation of the powers of darkness form a central core to the narrative of Jesus and deserve to be taken seriously by all those who claim to be understanding what impact the gospel narratives may have. They indicate that the career of Jesus is not about dealing with the symptoms of malaise but the very cause itself. We are dealing here not with individuals but a suprahuman power of evil which has led to individuals being cut off from their communities. Jesus' presence lays this bare and it is dealt with and the victims restored to wholeness. That is a power (*exousia*) which exceeds that of the scribes (Mark 1.22). We can be deceived into supposing that the problem lies in those possessed by unclean spirits. No, these are the indicators of the dislocation of the world. If you like they are barometers of the situation whose pervasive destructiveness extends into the lives of those who are regarded (and regard themselves) as 'normal'. Of course, as the gospel narrative indicates, it is precisely those who think they are normal and so have no need of repentance and restoration who are most profoundly deceived. The mystery of iniquity is so deep-seated that their insistence on the *status quo* leads them to take action against the one who has come to bind the strong man and to bring about liberation.

The growth of opposition from those who saw themselves as normal and rejected Jesus' claim to be a messianic prophet of the reign of God may help to explain his decision to go to Jerusalem.

Our gospels all stress that the journey to Jerusalem became central to his role as the agent of the kingdom of God. For the prophet of the reign of God it could not be otherwise; for it was impossible for a prophet to perish outside Jerusalem. Prophets, so the ancient traditions had asserted, had always suffered at the hands of their fellows. Elijah and Jeremiah had both paid heavily for their commitment to the ways of God. Jesus was to prove no exception.

To journey to Jerusalem, the seat of authority and economic power, was the act of a man who was aware of the political implications of his action. Jesus was no politician in any conventional sense. He was not, as far as we know a member of the Jewish Sanhedrin and stood outside the mainstream political processes. The reasons for this would not be too hard to seek. Politics in first-century Palestine concerned the task of achieving limited goals and preserving a modicum of freedom to pursue the worship of God. There was little if any room for messianic claimants in this process. Small wonder then that Jesus of Nazareth went up to Jerusalem and died as a martyr for the vision of the reign of God, a vision which he sought to implement as well as to proclaim. It was a vision which was ultimately rejected because the hierarchy in Jerusalem, wedded as it was to the Roman imperial system, preferred the compromises of the old order to the uncertainties and changes of the new. The maintenance of Temple worship was above all a reason for the hierarchy in Jerusalem to come to some accommodation with the Roman prefect. Caiaphas sought to guarantee that freedom to worship in the Temple by maintaining an uneasy relationship with the representative of Roman power. Challenges to the *status quo*, whether to Rome or Jewish High Priest, was to be viewed with suspicion and action taken.

In Jerusalem the Temple becomes a focus of Jesus' activity as prophet and teacher. First in an act reminiscent of the prophetic symbolic acts of old Jesus enters the house of God and overturns tables and casts out those who bought and sold in the outer court. Later he was to spend time preaching in the Temple precincts. Jesus was not the first to question the Temple practices. In the literature of the period there are several remarks expressing dissatisfaction with the Temple. We may suspect that Jesus and the first Christian martyr Stephen were not the first to express derogatory comments about it. There were some who regarded the Temple establishment as directly contrary to the divine will and took themselves off to the wilderness to maintain the true holiness in isolation waiting for the suitable time when a pure worship could be offered to God. Others like the Pharisees supported the Temple worship even if they were at odds with the hierarchy over details of practice. But meanwhile they worked a pattern of individual holiness which made ordinary existence an extension of Temple purity. It is not easy to understand the exact import of Jesus' words. Was he merely cleansing the Temple, or, as recent commentators have suggested, predicting its destruction and its replacement by the Temple of the new Age?

The use of the passage from Isaiah which speaks of the Temple as a house of prayer is remarkable. It might indicate a rejection of the sacrificial system based in the Temple which after all has no basis in the Torah. What is clear is that Jesus alludes to two passages which are firmly embedded in anti-Temple propaganda stemming from prophets of another age. He uses Jeremiah's words about the Temple being a 'den of thieves', uttered in the context of a stunning condemnation of the Temple and its ideology and the false reliance which was placed upon it. The universal promise of Isaiah 56.6f. may itself be part of the voice of protest of those who looked for a better and less narrow future for the people of God and eventually became so disillusioned that there is a strong criticism of the sacrificial system in Isaiah 66.1ff.

The message of doom on the Temple and the foreboding of a time when a terrible abomination of desolation would stand where he ought not to, come at the end of Jesus' career, if the narrative of the synoptics is followed. By that time opposition was widespread; the journey to Jerusalem had not led to national repentance, rather a plot by the hierarchy to kill Jesus. In such circumstances it would be no surprise that Jesus should predict judgment. After all, the one who believed himself to be the messiah was rejected by those who administered the shrine of God's presence. As in Ezekiel's day when the glory of God left a Temple destined to destruction, so too the divine glory manifested in the good news of the reign of God had been glimpsed elsewhere in the conquest of the powers as the messianic age was glimpsed. At the moment of the death of the messiah the veil which shrouded the holiest part of the Temple in mystery and awe was rent in two. It had become an empty shell; the glory had removed. Through the eyes of the soldier standing by, the Gospel of Mark leaves us in no doubt that the glory is found in the executed messiah: 'truly this man was the son of God'.

The synoptic gospels suggest that at the end of his life Jesus alluded in an enigmatic way to an uncertain future for his followers and prophesied a time of great tribulation. The certainty of vindication is there but the lot of the elect when they have been gathered from the four corners of the earth is not touched on at all in Mark. The element of judgment at the Parousia of the Son of Man is not entirely absent, however, from the synoptic discourses as the climax of the Matthean version is the account of the final asize with the Son of Man sitting on God's throne separating the sheep from the goats. But here as elsewhere in these discourses the focus of attention is on the present response of the elect. It is the recognition of the heavenly Son of Man in the brethren who are hungry, thirsty, strangers, naked, weak and imprisoned in the present age who will inherit the kingdom prepared by God from the foundation of the world.

Similarly in the Mark discourse the preoccupation of the bulk of the material is not so much the satisfaction of curiosity about the details of the times and seasons so much as dire warnings of the threat of being led astray, of failing at the last and of the need to be ready and watchful to avoid the worst of the disasters which are to come. In the bleak moments of the last days in Jerusalem there is little attempt to dwell on the privileges of discipleship. It is not a future without hope but the thoughts of the hearers are made to dwell on responsibilities in the short and medium term as the essential prerequisite of achieving a millennial bliss. In comparison with the more extended accounts of the coming of the new age to be found in other material, both Christian and Jewish, the synoptic discourses concentrate on the period of strife and tribulation leading up to the coming of the Son of Man; what happens thereafter is not explored.

It is easy to see how the discourse material in the gospels can be extracted from their narrative context and function as instructions which abstract the reader from the challenge of the messianic way as it intersects with an order which is passing away and into the world of fantastic speculation and out of touch with reality. The knowledge of the delights of Paradise and the horrors of Hell can lead to a morbid curiosity with the world beyond and the believer's participation in it, which can detract from the need to testify to the values of the reign of God in the injustice and oppression of an age which is passing away.

As has often been recognized we find differences among the gospels over the precision of the allusions. This is particularly evident in Mark 13.14 and parallels. Whereas Mark refers cryptically to the abomination of desolation standing where he ought not, Matthew has a more explicit link with the book of Daniel (ch. 11) where the allusion is to the erection of a statue in the Temple by the Syrian king Antiochus IV. Matthew has this in mind in his reference to the holy place; Luke has an explicit prediction of a historical event, the destruction of Jerusalem. On the basis of Markan priority and the dependence of Matthew and Luke on Mark we may find here an example of the developing historical specificity as the eschatological discourse was used. The interpretative possibilities which are left open by the text of Mark are circumscribed in both Matthew and Luke. The reader's imagination is indeed given full rein by the Mark text whereas he/she is directed to a much narrower range of interpretative possibilities in Matthew and Luke.

The eschatological discourse in the synoptic gospels must not be separated from the narrative of Jesus' proclamation and inauguration of the reign of God. It is that context which is necessary to prevent the discourse about the future becoming the goal of the narrative. Discipleship involves sharing the way of the cross of the son of man as he goes up to Jerusalem. What is offered the disciple is the sharing of the cup of suffering of the son of man rather than the promise of sitting at his right hand and his left when he reigns on earth. It is not that this request is repudiated but, as the eschatological discourse makes plain, there can be no escape from the painful reality of the present witness with its need to endure the tribulations which precede the vindication. That is the challenge which faces those who wish to live out the messianic narrative in their own lives; no short cuts to the messianic reign are to be found here. Jesus promises his disciples persecution and the need to be ready to bear witnesses before the courts of the powerful. They can expect to maintain a critical distance from the institutions of the old order. The decisive question is not so much 'How can I survive this situation with the least possible harm?' . . . Rather, the one question which is important is: 'In this situation, how can one bear witness to the way of the Messiah?'[1] When the abomination of desolation appears, there is a summons to an exodus. Life along the usual lines is no longer a realistic option for the disciple who must be ready to flee to the mountains. The consequence is social separation and a refusal to join in the normal pattern of society.

The language of hope itself offers an alternative perspective on the arrangements of the present. A broader horizon is offered and the reader is asked to consider the present in the light of the threat of judgment and the glory of the age to come. It is this alternative vision to which the apocalyptic and millenarian tradition has borne witness. It has protested against those arrangements which have the appearance of order but which in reality have brought about the prosperity and progress of some at the expense of others. It is frequently those who have to bear that suffering who can see the fragility of those structures which appear to offer peace and security. Those whose lives are fragmented and who live at the margins can discern the signs of the times in ways which are frightening to those of us who cannot see from what is apparently a more favoured vantage-point.

It is the attentiveness to the context of the eschatological predictions which may help us towards some kind of guidelines with regard to their usage. We are confronted with a variety of symbols open to bewildering and often bizarre interpretations. We have been content to cope with this in various ways. First, by concentrating on the eschatological interpretation we can make the material irrelevant to our contemporary mundane concerns. Those who read these symbols in such a way that they relate to present circumstances are charged with illegitimate use of the material. Secondly, we find something similar happening within mainstream biblical interpretation. We are told that attention to the original context would reveal that the text cannot relate to present circumstances and events. A glance at the book of Daniel would enable us to see that the abomination of desolation referred to something in the Temple in Jerusalem and not to present threats to the people of

God. But is it quite as simple as all that? Does the Gospel of Mark allow us so easily to interpret the enigmatic passage so easily with either past or future circumstances? The gospel addresses us as readers: '*Let the reader understand*'. If only we have eyes to see, we can make sense. And many throughout history have been attentive to that summons as they have sought to see the abomination of desolation and the marks of the beast around them. They perceive that this generation is faced with a challenge which it ignores at its peril.

The contemporary preacher may look at Mark 13.14 and, if s/he needs inspiration for a contemporary denunciation of wickedness, be tempted to equate this with institutions preparing nuclear arms, or bases where the aircraft or missiles to carry these weapons of mass destruction are stored. The historical purist may retort: 'Jesus could not have this in mind'. But the question is: what *did* he have in mind? Surely, a mistaken exegesis would be one which reduced the meaning of the abomination of desolation to the places where weapons of destruction may be produced. What is spoken of here is the manifestation of an ultimate incarnation of wickedness. But even if we cannot identify the abomination of desolation with Aldermaston, or Upper Heyford or even the Ministry of Defence, we cannot separate these institutions where power is being used to limit, suppress and destroy, from the symbol of sacrilege and desolation spoken of in the gospel. As we seek to follow the pattern of Jesus' life in the lives of the people of God today, there will be occasions when manifestations of that kind of wickedness which is an affront to God's purposes may confront us and the abomination of desolation cast its shadow on our lives.

Our Christian ancestors did not hesitate to find in the iniquities of their companions the marks of the eschatological agents whose way was opposed to Christ and to address them as such. Those who failed to love their brothers and sisters are Antichrists (I John 2.20). If we recognize that institutions created by fallible men and women in the interests of power are all implicitly demonic and can assume supra-human and sub-human proportions when that power is abused and humanity threatened, then we shall be less squeamish about using passages like Mark 13 which so offend our liberal conscience. What is being condemned here is not merely an individual but a symbol of the distorting power of evil. It is what followers of Jesus in every generation should learn to see and to name, for there can be no accommodation with that which promotes the opposite of all that Jesus and the way of the cross stand for.

The problem in 'demonizing' one's opponents is that it suggests a self-righteous confidence in one's own credentials for theological perception and rectitude. The condemnation of the 'antichrists' in I John needs to be tempered by the frank recognition by the author: 'If we say that *we* have no sin we deceive ourselves and the truth is not in us'. We do not live in a perfect world and those who claim the spirit of God must always recognize that they live in the time of the overlap of the ages; the reign of God has not yet arrived and the fallibility of the old order affects the judgment of the saints as well as those outside the church. Saying this can lead to an unwillingness to confront evil in our midst, because we feel we can never be sure. Confronting the powers, however, *is* an important part of our task, but it remains dangerously incomplete if we are seeking to exorcise the demons elsewhere without recognizing them in ourselves. That honesty of self-knowledge which can be fostered within the supportive community is an essential part of the process of discerning the shadow cast by the abomination of desolation in our contemporary world.

Whereas Jesus, the son of Ananias would have perished without trace if it had not been for the historian Josephus, the story of the prophet from Nazareth was kept alive by those who were convinced that not only his message but that he had survived. Of course, even within the early church that sense of urgency and the impending critical moment passed. Although Paul could echo Jesus' conviction that the critical moment had come: now is the acceptable time; now is the day of salvation. That eschatological conviction waned and the arena of the eschatological salvation focussed on individual and the community of the elect. It was a way of keeping alive the messianic vision in less than hospitable times. But the power of the imagery and the breadth of the vision could never be wholly contained and prompted successors who have had the eyes to see the fragility and folly of arrangements in their world.

That process of utilizing those images continues to this day. We cannot deny that identification is being made. Are we to condemn that process as entirely illegitimate or, worse still, act as if it was not happening by distancing ourselves from these ambivalent symbols and looking for more congenial parts of the biblical tradition for our consolation? In his last discourse in which the threat of the future formed the substance of Jesus' advice to his disciples there were dire warnings about the embodiment of evil which was opposed, resisted and shunned. Nothing could be more evil than the threat of nuclear annihilation. However well-intentioned those people are who seek to preserve peace by nuclear deterrence, we have to ask ourselves again and again: what are they seeking to preserve? Who has most to lose in this country? The uncomfortable answer to those questions is that deterrence, like military might throughout the centuries, preserves the position of those who already manoeuvre the levers of power. In the light of this the advice of Jesus is unequivocal: 'the person who seeks to save their life will lose it and the one who loses life for my sake and for the gospel will find it . . . the kings of the earth lord over it over their subjects and their mighty, men are called benefactors *it shall not be so among you . . .*'

----------------------------------(5)----------------------------------

The Armageddon Scenario

Mark Corner

The 'Peace Movements' that have built up in the West over the last ten years have made us all more aware of how complete a devastation would be wrought upon the world by a nuclear war – even a 'small' one – and of how possible (if not probable) it is that we shall experience this devastation within our lifetimes. The 'Nuclear Age' became self-conscious in the 1980s. From 'The War Game', rescued from BBC censorship, through the more up-dated version of a nuclear attack in 'Threads', to the Oxford Union debate between Caspar Weinberger and E. P. Thompson, the issue of nuclear warfare (and also that of nuclear power) has been the subject of drama, debate and endless studio discussion for the past decade or so. Some of the media coverage has, of course, been very poor. But it has had its effect. The British Government may or may not have been influenced by CND to agree that cruise missiles should be removed from Greenham Common and Molesworth (cynics might say that they are being transferred on to ships where they are less vulnerable to attack). But they have certainly been influenced to cancel or downplay those civil defence manoeuvres that Willie Whitelaw used to enthuse about in the early 1980s. No one is now reassured by 'Protect and Survive'. Few are now either expectant or desirous of surviving nuclear attack. The Peace Movement may have failed to convince the nation that their methods are the right ones for avoiding war, but they have managed to convince it of the horror of modern warfare itself.

'The Nuclear Age' in its period of self-conscious awareness that accidents may happen, bombs may proliferate, world leaders may grow senile or lose their tempers, and regional conflicts may escalate into world war, has not shown any confidence in an end to such dangers. Perhaps the agreement between Reagan and Gorbachev marks a welcome new era of commitment to reducing the prospect of war, but so far fear, insecurity and fatalistic acceptance have been the common reaction to the removal of the bomb from a list of nationally taboo subjects. A minority has been enthusiastic about its peace-keeping qualities; a majority has simply felt that what has been invented cannot be dis-invented, and that the weapon once discovered must be with us for ever. Like the weather, it can be complained about but not resisted, and unlike the weather no precautions can be taken against it. Like much else that has characterized the political complexion of Britain in the 1980s, there is little enthusiasm but even less opposition. Nothing, it is believed, can be done about it, and anything that was done would only make things worse. Such fatalism allows the minority who wholeheartedly support the Bomb, and even invest a lot of national pride in it, to carry the rest along with it in the absence of any alternative.

Theology in this nuclear age has a choice. It can go with the fatalistic tide or against it. If it goes with it, it can develop apocalyptic ideas to give the prevailing mood of fatalism a religious flavour, and sanction with a Christian vision of Armageddon the expectation of nuclear catastrophe. Alternatively, it can go against the tide. It can find in this world something to love, preserve and improve. It can call for a this-worldly justice and peace in which the cry is 'Thy will be done on earth as it is in heaven', rather than 'Thy will be done by the destruction of the earth'. In contemporary religious writing one can find both points of view.

The former viewpoint has been examined by the writer Gore Vidal in a collection of essays entitled *Armageddon?* The essay which donates its title to the book[1] described the attitude of Fundamentalist Christians in America who offer a 'religious' interpretation of contemporary history. According to their understanding, events such as the formation of the state of Israel, the rise of the Common Market in Europe (viewed as a rebirth of the Roman Empire), and the development into great powers this century of the Soviet Union and China, are all predicted in the

53

Bible. Not only that, but the fulfilment of these biblical 'predictions' means that we live in the 'penultimate Dispensation', a period immediately preceding the final confrontation between the forces of Christ and anti-Christ at Armageddon. This will be the highlight of a series of terrible events that involve the destruction of the world as we know it. However, true believers will be spared such horrors through the 'Rapture', an interpretation of Paul's first letter to the Thessalonians 4.17 which describes an evacuation of the followers of Christ to 'meet the Lord in the air', away from the earthly perils taking place.

Such millenarian musings are not always taken very seriously in Britain, where Fundamentalist Christianity usually takes a less extreme form, but their significance can be under-estimated as well as exaggerated. They are widely known in the United States through the works of retired riverboat captain Hal Lindsey and others. His *The Late Great Planet Earth* was among the best-selling non-fiction (sic) works of the 1970s, and Lindsey has renewed his ideas for the new decade in *The 1980s: Countdown to Armageddon*. The readership for such books, and numerous others like them, runs into millions, and extends throughout American society, right up to a President who exercised effective control over the destiny of the world for eight years.[2]

If we are tempted not to take seriously the flirtation with such ideas both across the Atlantic and, increasingly, over here, then I think that we should at least consider why it is taking place. It surely functions as a form of religious response to the fear and insecurity felt by men and women in a world which, I have argued, they increasingly perceive to be threatened by destruction. The sense of nuclear weapons as a threat to, rather than guarantee of, peace, produces an uneasy calm of helplessness and living in the moment. The world is out of control, but at least we have a chance of enjoying its technological fruits for a little longer before those fruits themselves, in the form of nuclear technology, turn sour and destroy us. The sense of progress, of slow development towards wisdom through the generations, is broken by the awareness that a planet with so many untriggered nuclear devices is bound at some point or other to self-destruct. Things are out of control.

In such circumstances, we reach for an alternative vision. Perhaps what is out of our control may nevertheless be within God's. Perhaps even if we cannot save ourselves, God himself can save us. Better to know that the worst will happen, but that at least in doing so it's all in the hands of God, than to recognize that things are out of everyone's control, whether human or divine. The Armageddon scenario may seem totally unattractive. It is not. At least it offers a pattern, a way of fitting fragmentary human life and uncontrollable technological progress into a theme of over-arching divine control. Better to know that 'He's got the whole world in his hands,' even if he's going to bring them together and crush it. The advantage of interpreting biblical prophecy as 'prediction' is that it makes it seem that the key to all that has happened and will happen can be placed in our hands. We can unlock the mysteries of the universe, and replace anxiety that we cannot order the world to a good purpose with surrender to the divine will.

One can see exactly the same temptation with other contemporary crises like AIDS. Those who refuse to believe that we can cure this illness ourselves, both through medical technology and through changed patterns of behaviour, adopt a view that it is God's will and that we must surrender to whatever form the divine 'punishment' takes. Such a view may rest less on a particular biblical interpretation or theological principle than on a psychological need. Fear and insecurity turn to anything or anyone that can impose order on the chaos. It is no good complaining that such views make God into a tyrant. A tyrant is precisely what, in the circumstances, a lot of people want.

Understanding the Armageddon scenario fully would benefit from an historical study of other periods when a lack of social cohesion and personal security have spawned visions of an imminent divinely-initiated end to the world. Some see parallels with the break-up of medieval society, racked by its own health hazard in the form of the Black Death, and characterized by profound changes as the feudal ice broke and that unitary political and social order, Christendom, gave way to the nation-state and capitalist enterprise. Such comparisons have to be treated very carefully, particularly where changes that took place sporadically over centuries are concerned. But it is important to put the sort of speculation which appears to be increasingly in evidence today into historical context.[3]

Indeed, it needs to be remembered that Christianity was a religion which from the very beginning faced uncertainty about the nature of Christ's return. Many biblical scholars think that Paul himself had to come to terms with an unexpected delay in the Parousia. The question of Jesus' own attitude has also been taken up in this century by, among others, Albert Schweitzer in *The Quest of the Historical Jesus*. From the outset, then, Christianity has had the difficult task of understanding the place of eschatology, the doctrine of the 'last things', within an overall theological scheme from the world's creation to its consummation. To some extent, the 'Armageddon' interpretation provides an unsatisfactory solution to what remains for many Christians a problem, namely whether and in what sense Christ's Second Coming can be explained.

It may seem from what I have said so far that a very negative image of apocalyptic expectation (in the sense described) is being offered, as if it were a distraction which distorted the minds of Christians – perhaps even that of the founder of Christianity – and prevented the development of a Christian ethic and philosophy based upon a firm commitment to the indefinite existence of this world. Certainly, the language of apocalyptic can also be a means of protest, of rebellion against an unjust political order in the present, a role which it arguably plays, for instance, in the Book of Revelation. But we are not talking here of a vision that expresses the longing for another social order on earth. We are certainly not talking of anything so positive, so man-made, as rebellion. We are talking of events being taken out of the hands of human beings, who find themselves unable to direct them, and handed over instead to God, who can direct them instead to their (literal) end. We are pointing to the voluntary self-immolation of men and women who have given up hope of directing their lives or those of their communities towards anything recognizable as human progress. Instead they surrender everything to Another who will act on their behalf. Tyranny is so much less demanding than anarchy.

In his classic work *The Fear of Freedom* Erich Fromm tried to understand the motives that might lead men and women to prefer subjection to independence.[4] His view was that subjection brought a form of security which independence, in a world without any clear sense of direction, did not. Fromm's understanding of the success of tyrants, whether divine ones like the predestining God of Calvin's imagination or human ones like Hitler, was that their appeal lay not in what they commanded but in the fact that they commanded. They produced an overarching order within which everyone had a clear role to play, including of course that of victim. Their demonic metaphysics are preferable to the inconclusive suggestions of their opponents.

In such circumstances, freedom ceases to be a good, for freedom suggests human responsibility and the need for men and women to admit that they, and no one else, are responsible for what happens in the world. It is hard to admit that if events are out of control, the reason is that human beings have not tried hard enough to control them for themselves. And it is hard to accept that if our failure does bring catastrophe of nuclear proportions, then such an outcome can never be viewed as anything other than a tragedy. For the human race would have failed and have let down its creator. Stewardship of the earth would have proved beyond its capacity.

On the other hand, if this human control is a mere illusion, and the hand of God steers human history on our behalf, then even the end of the world appears no longer a tragic mistake, a terrible human error, but a further illustration of God's plan. He (or even she) who presses the button becomes the instrument of God's will. They can genuinely say at any heavenly Nuremberg trial: 'We were only obeying orders' – in this case those of the creator himself as recorded in scripture. The probable outcome of history no longer serves as a terrible indictment of the human race, but as the fulfilment of God's will, in which men and women played their crucial if subordinate role.

The Armageddon scenario has attractions not only because a simplistic biblical interpretation is often hard to refute, but also because it expresses a deep-seated psychological need, one which ironically has been partly unleashed by the one success which the peace movements can claim unequivocally to have had – that of awakening us to the dangers of all things nuclear. To counter it, Christians have to develop a theology of the nuclear age which puts into reverse many of the assumptions of the 'Armageddon' position. In particular, it has to emphasize the role of men and women as active determinants of the social order, bound by their

Christianity to submit neither to a God who does everything on their behalf, nor to 'principalities and powers' that must be obeyed whatever form they might take.

Indeed, these two forms of submission are closely linked. Much of Christian thought has tended to suggest that the social and political order of the day is a divine 'order of creation', which human beings must submit to whatever its nature. If it is a good social order it is a divine blessing; if it is an evil social order it is a form of divine chastisement. Such an attitude may be more characteristic of some forms of Christianity than others – more Lutheran than Calvinist, for instance – but it has informed all Christian traditions that participate in the Constantinian legacy of collusion with the dominant socio-political order. Such teaching instructs Christians that rather than resist oppression they must endure it, and suffer it not so much as a punishment from their fellow-human beings as a scourge from God. Like the régimes to which God was wont to subject the Israelites in the Old Testament when they proved disobedient, all tyrannical forms of government come to be understood as agents of divine wrath. On this understanding, just as God led the people of Israel out of their oppression in Egypt, so he will lead the people of any oppressed nation out of bondage only when his will so orders it. In the meantime, they should not anticipate his decision.

It is this interpretation of human history as a direct expression of God's will, into which human beings have no input as co-operating agents, that lies behind the ease with which many receive the general tenor – if not the detailed exegesis – of the 'Armageddon' scenario today. Centuries of tradition telling Christians that whatever social and political order they live under is an expression of God's will leads naturally enough to the assumption that the present global order, even as it lurches towards destruction, must be an expression of that divine purpose. The security of knowing that everything is under God's control replaces the commitment to make every human effort to manage society better at a critical moment of history.

When the Cambridge psychologist Nicholas Humphrey gave the Richard Dimbleby lecture on a hesitant BBC earlier in this decade, he spoke of the incapacity of the human imagination to comprehend a nuclear disaster. Before such a catastrophe the mind is mesmerized by shock, unable to comprehend it. It is frozen like an animal hypnotized by a snake. If it is capable of any reaction, it is akin to primeval awe. Here are the basic elements of the universe revealing their awesome power. The last thing that comes to its mind is the need to react, to assert mastery, to control the forces of technology rather than be controlled by them. Instead, the mind adopts a protective passivity akin to the amnesia of an accident victim who cannot bear to recall painful or tragic circumstances in the past. Something so dauntingly powerful, released to threaten the very existence of civilization, can only be ignored. It would be too painful to try to resist it.[5]

Yet the Soviet Union, in the wake of Chernobyl, has tried to control the primeval forces unleashed by that disaster. It is perhaps difficult for us to comprehend, even though we have felt the fallout ourselves, what such a disaster must have meant to that nation. Mikhail Gorbachev has appeared on the world stage with little room for manoeuvre, facing a partially hostile Politburo and public at home, and a largely sceptical audience abroad. If he pursues a policy of aggression, he is yet another Russian bent on world domination; if he pursues a policy of reconciliation, he is a subtle operator able to cloak his designs. A conspiracy thesis is available to put a bad interpretation on every conceivable Soviet move. Yet it remains extraordinary that he has already achieved some impact upon the West. If it is too much to expect the West to see in his attempt to ban all nuclear tests a determination to give no further opportunity – even those of a 'controlled' kind – for nuclear forces to unleash themselves as they did so tragically at Chernobyl, still his commitment to rid the world of nuclear weapons has at least been noted, and a start made on the process of disarmament (as opposed to the controlled rearmament of previous East-West accords). As an atheist (we presume), he is denied the possibility of seeing in nuclear weapons a possible instrument of divine chastisement. His commitment must necessarily be to the preservation of this present world-order, by asserting the capacity of human reason and will to manage even the products of nuclear technology. In some ways, that makes him a more desirable leader for a superpower than his opponent. As Gore Vidal remarked to Norman Mailer:

I think there should be a Constitutional amendment making it impossible for anyone to be president who believes in an after-life.[6]

It was a cynical remark, but one can see its logic.

But should it not be precisely the Christian world leader who is committed to the abolition of those forces which threaten to destroy all that humanity has attempted to make of the world entrusted to it by God? Should not those who claim to be leaders of 'Christian' nations, or who are themselves Christians, be the ones who express the determination to transform this world into a society fit to survive in?

This brings us to the very different reaction to living in a nuclear age offered by a contemporary Christian movement whose principles differ completely from those of the 'Armageddon' theorists, namely the movement or set of movements which could be grouped together under the heading of the Theology of Liberation. Within this school of thought, the prophets of the Old Testament do not 'predict' future events as if they are reading the divine tea leaves for what must inevitably take place. Rather, prophecy is very closely linked to protest. The prophets challenge the social injustice of their day, and Jesus himself, recognizing the way in which the prophets were persecuted before him (Matt. 23.31–32, 37), knew that such a challenge was dangerous. Amos, Hosea, Jeremiah and Jesus himself stand in a line of prophecy which has criticized the *status quo* and called for radical action in the face of current trends, many of them complacently upheld. They called upon Israel to make God's will a reality on earth, to end the injustice which neglected the orphan and widow or threw up great disparities of wealth between rich and poor. Each prophet presumed that it was in the hands of men and women to change society, to make it conform more to the will of its creator. This presumption was not denied by the fact that a warning of God's wrath or a promise of God's blessing might be given alongside the exhortation to change. For while judgment ultimately is God's, this in no way undercuts human responsibility to act in the world now. Liberation theology, in the words of Philip Berryman, 'gives . . . a transformative rather than a fatalistic stance toward the world'.[7]

Such an interpretation of prophecy is anthithetical to that of the 'Armageddon' Fundamentalists. For the latter no longer wish to hear of human responsibility, only of what God is going to do on their behalf. The prophets become fortune tellers informing humanity of what is bound to happen to it. We should not be too surprised at this. A great deal of popular interest in religion is of a fatalistic kind. Horoscopes, tarot cards, the burgeoning interest in the occult – all are at least partly to do with the premise that the future is to be seen but not made. People attempt to peer into their future as if it is a ready-made object about to fall on to their heads. What the Armageddon scenario offers is a glimpse of the future of the world, a horoscope for humanity, one that commands nothing except acceptance. Rather than seeing the vision of humanity's destruction as a warning of the consequences for men and women of failing to do God's will, it becomes itself God's will, the unalterable divine plan for the world. The real purpose of prophecy, to goad a complacent people into change, is thus turned on its head. Prophecy instead becomes an encouragement to fatalistic acceptance that what will be will be.

For Jesus of Nazareth, the warning of destruction was always based upon a failure of God's people to respond:

> Then he began to upbraid the cities where most of his mighty works had been done, because they did not repent. 'Woe to you, Chora'zin! Woe to you, Beth-sa'ida! For if the mighty works done in you had been done in Tyre and Sidon, they would have repented long ago in sackcloth and ashes. But I tell you, it shall be more tolerable on the day of judgment for Tyre and Sidon than for you.' (Matt. 11.20–22)

Any vision of the power of God to destroy the world is linked to a failure of God's people to repent. The point of prophecy is to encourage such repentance, incorporating a suggestion of future suffering as a means of rousing a nation to repentance. The threat in Jeremiah 4.23ff., in which the prophet has a vision of the earth once again returned to the state of being 'waste and void', the primeval chaos out of which God created a cosmos (Gen. 1.2), is entirely based upon a people's failure to turn to their Creator. So much so, that God sends Jeremiah running through the streets of Jerusalem in the hope of finding someone that 'does justice and seeks truth; that I may pardon her' (Jer.5.1).

In the nuclear age, however, there are many who want to turn every Jeremiah into a Cassandra. Faced by a world within which forces are unleashed that are beyond our control, above all the power of nuclear technology, it appears to many that a return to the 'primeval chaos' is inevitable. The most that can be sought is an assurance that the destruction humanity faces is the design of an all-powerful God rather than the tragic error of an incompetent and malicious human race. Rather like those intercessory prayers in which the priest announces that 'we lay before God' all the misery, suffering and stupidity of humanity – a kind of perverse reversal of the concept of sacrifice! – we are prone to lay before God the most dangerous weapon in our history, and attempt to turn it into his weapon rather than our own.

What our theology must surely become, in the face of 'Armageddon', is empowering. It must encourage men and women with the Christian message that they are co-workers with God in building the kingdom of God here on earth. This message has too often been supplanted by a more fatalistic suggestion that they are to eke out an existence on earth before entering the kingdom in the life to come. In the 1980s, we have become aware in the West of being affected by much that seems totally beyond our control. International capital ebbs and flows from bull market to bear, like a worldwide tide that can no more be interfered with than Canute could stop the waves. Unemployment has swept into Britain, again like an international force that is now seen, rightly or wrongly, as beyond our control, something to regret like bad weather but not to get angry and protest about. Into this context fits the most serious international force of all, nuclear power, proliferating weapons around the globe and threatening the end of civilization. None of these forces that affects our lives so seriously appears to be capable of management, even on a governmental level.

From a quite different perspective, however, socialist nations do claim to be able to exercise such management. Whether or not an implication of such control is an intolerable interference with human freedom, a state like the Soviet Union claims the authority to control employment and capital on behalf of its people. The tragedy of Chernobyl showed that there was still the uncontrollable force of nuclear power, and the experience arguably administered a shock to the Soviet system. It is the Russians who now take the lead in arguing that nuclear weapons must not only be reduced but eliminated. Men and women must control technology and not be controlled by it. They have the power to order the world for good rather than evil, and should take responsibility for using it.

In a Western context, where government is all too often seen as a burden on people's backs rather than a means of securing a good way of life, such confidence is often lacking. By way of contrast, it is in the Third World that the theology of liberation has more successfully been able to give Christians a sense of power over their own destinies. Through practical initiatives within the 'base communities', such as literacy campaigns, co-operatives, and the development of grievance procedures, attempts are made to give men and women a greater control over their own lives. The process of 'conscientization' (consciousness-raising) seeks to be a means by which people receive for themselves the power to be agents of their own progress.

The function of theology as enabling, both for individuals and at a corporate level for national communities, is equally important for the First World. I have tried to suggest that the threat of nuclear war casts a fatalistic shadow over our lives, one that is rather different from the helplessness engendered by the absolute poverty of many citizens in Latin America or Africa. It is a threat that may reach deeper into our psyches than we like to recognize. The Western Peace Movements have succeeded in raising our consciousness to the horrors of nuclear war and the impracticability of defending ourselves in the face of a nuclear attack, but they have been less successful in inspiring us to take bold measures to lessen the danger of such an attack in the first place. In such circumstances, the danger is that they have only reinforced a sense of helplessness, one that seems equally prevalent in the face of powerful economic and social forces that oppress us at the same time.

In our own First World society there is a sense of powerlessness felt within an industrially advanced community. Such a society needs its own form of liberation theology. Technology, seen a century ago as the servant of progress, is viewed by many in our own age as a runaway force dominating rather than dominated by the communities that possess it. It is crucial that we recover a sense of human responsibility for the world we live in. In Latin America, it may be social and economic deprivation, coupled with threats of physical brutality, that frustrates that recovery. In the First World, it is in part the over-arching shadow of something immense and uncontrollable that we have unwittingly released but cannot master, the genie that has been let out of the bottle. In both societies, the Christian message must be the same; not that of subservience to evil powers that are rationalized as God's will, but of resistance to forces that frustrate both human progress and the purposes of God. Such may not be the theology of our political or religious leaders, but we have our own base communities within which a true theology can be developed, and never was there a greater need of it than now.

Boldness in Spirituality

6

Reasons for not Despairing

Rex Ambler

Insofar as a nuclear war poses a threat of death for each of us it challenges us to discover again the sources of hope that enable us to face our own death. Insofar as it poses a threat of extinction to the human race as a whole it seems to cut off every source of hope we might turn to. If the human race is made extinct there will be, for example, no future in which the wrongs of the present can be righted, no discernible meaning to the human project as a whole, no possibility of any good purpose for the world, even God's, being carried through to fruition. The world would end with the greatest possible eruption of evil without the least possible opportunity for redemption. For those who have already despaired of the world there may perhaps be, or seem to be, a shadowy hope that their souls will survive the destructive event – but what kind of bliss they can envisage for themselves with the knowledge of that event is impossible to imagine. For those who still cherish the world – because they belong to it or in it, or because, despite the evil in the world, they know God's presence in it – such a prospect is almost unthinkable. I say unthinkable because to try to think of the end of the world is like trying to think of the end of one's life, but without the benefit of knowing that others will live on after to help give it sense. To try to think of the end as a destructive and evil event with no hope of redress is to undermine any confidence that goodness has any point at all. (In this respect Christians would seem to be no better off than anyone else, since up till now they have always expressed *some* hope for this world.) And finally, to try to think of the end as an irredeemable evil that we ourselves would have helped to bring about – however tenuous and complex, our responsibility in this is inescapable – is to envisage a guilt that is too great to bear, and for which no comparable forgiveness can even be conceived. The event itself is both obscure and opaque: we cannot properly think about it, nor can we think beyond it to a future that could make sense of it. It is in every respect an end, a boundary of our world, beyond which is only a darkness that stretches to infinity.

We can of course dearly hope that such an event will never occur. We can also support that hope by describing the forces of sanity and good will which are at work in the world to prevent such a thing happening, and by adding our own effort to the cause. But such a hope is not to be understood as a confidence about the future, certainly not the confidence of religious faith. It is a weaker, paler kind of hope, the hope of a wish, or perhaps of an optimistic calculation. But even optimism has to be qualified as never before, for the risk of things not going as hoped – and even the optimist has to accept that risk – is the risk of losing everything. When the whole machinery of death is in place, when nothing remains to be done to set it in motion but for a few politicians to make a few big 'mistakes', how is it possible to calculate an optimistic outcome? Even people actively committed to the abolition of the nuclear machinery know their efforts may not succeed, but that in the last resort insanity and irresponsibility might prevail. Indeed that dark knowledge is what gives such urgency to the movement for abolition. At the same time it gives, or may give, a sense of futility to their efforts, for as long as the possibility of war hangs over them, and with it the possibility of human extinction, it is possible that their efforts will be wholly ineffective. A nuclear holocaust will be 'no respecter of persons'; it will fall on the just and the unjust alike.

By the same token, any good cause whatever, whether aimed at disarmament or not, will be caught within the same futility. Every long term project we work for, every good thing we believe in that we hope will bear fruit in time is threatened by the mere possibility that at any time it could all be wiped out. And since everything we do is inspired by some hope, however nebulous, everything we do is potentially futile. In this way the dark threat that looms on our horizon casts a long, dark shadow over the whole of human life.

It might appear though that Christians at least have a basis for hope because they believe in the God on which the world itself depends. They can surely feel confident, we might think, that whatever humans do to their world God is able to save it, indeed that God *will* save it since he has already committed himself to it both in creating it and in redeeming it through Christ. (Some Christians have pointed to the promise of the covenant with Noah as a specific basis for this hope: 'I will never again curse the ground because of man, for the imagination of his heart is evil from his youth; neither will I again destroy every living creature as I have done', Gen. 8.21; cf. 9.8–17.) The assumption is that God is able to intervene in history and redirect it according to his will, and that if and when his own purpose for history is threatened he will most certainly do so. The assumption seems natural enough within the context of a traditional Christian faith, but when applied to the present nuclear situation it begins to look very shaky indeed. We could suppose for example that God would bring influence to bear on our world leaders through their advisers or through popular protest so that they would freely decide never to press the nuclear button. Yet this would not be sufficient. Quite apart from the practical point that a decision of that sort would undermine the deterrence policy and effectively remove the leaders concerned from office, there is the logical point that God cannot *force* people to act *freely* in accordance with his will, and that therefore God cannot guarantee a particular outcome. So if we believe that God has in fact guaranteed the safety of the world – and that our hope in God depends on this guarantee – we must also believe that God must act, when the occasion requires, to stop human beings from doing what they have freely set out to do. If he cannot act effectively *through* them because they are unresponsive, he must act against them to crush their freedom. If we suppose then that our leaders have freely decided to launch a nuclear attack, there are a limited number of ways in which God could be thought to stop them. He could prevent them physically from pressing the button. Or, if the button had been pressed, he could at the last moment act as a supernatural nuclear shield to stop the launched weapons in mid-flight. Or thirdly, we could suppose, as 'dispensationalists' do, that God will miraculously rescue them from the impending disaster by removing all true believers from the earth – to return again with

Christ for his promised reign on earth. (I will not discuss the question of how life on earth is envisaged *after* a nuclear holocaust, but suggest only that those in doubt should read Jonathan Schell's *The Fate of the Earth*.) But when we spell it out in this detail it is clear that in the process of trying to rescue hope God has been reduced to a quasiphysical force, an invisible Superman, and that faith in God accordingly has become a superstitious fantasy. It is perhaps understandable that in the face of such an awesome prospect as nuclear annihilation people will look to God as the all-powerful parent to save them from trouble, and that in childish desperation they will let all sense of reality go.

More serious than such infantile fantasy, however, is the profounder denial of our human responsibility in the situation. Perhaps the childish regression is itself a psychological device for evading the solemn call to responsibility that comes to us through the nuclear situation. To suppose either that God will prevent a war or that God will rescue believers from it is to deny the fact of our own new-found collective power. Whether through a wilful refusal to look facts in the face or through an innocent ignorance of the modern world they have denied an important, perhaps *the* important, reality of our time. If such denial is the price of religious faith today we might be led to believe that we should be better off, and much safer, without it.

Faith does not have to take this form, however. It can indeed take the opposite form of a trust in reality itself, however harsh and threatening it might be. It can trust reality in its harshness to teach us and purify us, and reality in its goodness to enrich us and redeem us. It can take everything that comes to us, even failure and death, as a means of grace, that is, as a way of connecting us with the ultimate source of our being, where we find the alienations and isolations of our self-centred lives overcome. It is a faith that abandons (little by little, maybe) the evasions of a supernatural world and the illusions of an absolute security in this world. It derives its confidence, not from promises of protection against all possible danger, but from knowledge of a reality deeper than our individual selves which can give us an unshakable identity.

Such, I believe, was the faith of Jesus, a faith he also urged on his followers. It was a faith that abjured all pre-planned scenarios – 'even the Son of Man knows not the time . . .' – and expressed itself in the willingness to let go worldly security in the voluntary acceptance of suffering and possible death. That faith was projected on to the future, not as a prediction of events beyond human control, but, quite the contrary, as an acceptance of a new possibility which depended precisely (but not only) on human beings for its realization. The 'kingdom of God' was 'near', for those who could see it, waiting for them to seek it and enter it. In this way Jesus' teaching was wholly in line with the tradition of prophecy which had insisted that the promised day of blessing would arrive *only if* the people were faithful to their God; if they weren't faithful that day would be a time of great suffering, a judgment rather than a blessing.

That kind of faith is exactly what is called for by the present crisis of international security, which to a remarkable degree echoes the crisis of Jesus' own time. There is now, as then, a threat to the stability of our world from the blind and arrogant pretensions of power, from the 'kingdoms of this world'. The 'signs' are there. If we support these pretensions of power, even to the extent of meekly accepting what others do in our name, we shall help to bring the world to an end, and in doing so we shall 'lose our own souls'. If we refuse to support them and choose instead to live our lives and order our affairs out of a profounder trust in God, we shall be helping to bring about a whole human order which could indeed be called 'the kingdom of God' since it would not be structured around *human* pretensions of sovereignty and power. In such a commitment, even in the event that it led to our death, our 'souls' would have been saved – our lives indeed would have gained an eternal significance because they were lived out of and for the eternal reality that gave us existence.

There is of course an important respect in which our situation is different from the situations of Jesus and the Hebrew prophets, a respect in which, we have to say, it is wholly new and unprecedented. It is the fact that our power to destroy the world has increased to the extent that it can destroy life itself, destroy even the possibility that human beings would survive in any state at all. The threatened 'world' of Jesus' time was the humanly constructed order of society. It was conceivable that if *that* world were destroyed, human beings would still survive and that through them

71

and with them God would establish a new world. But the 'world' that is under threat in our time is much larger than that. It embraces virtually the whole life of the earth. If this world were destroyed there would be no such possibility of survival and renewal.

The difference is crucial for the form that Christian hope can assume in our time. The nuclear reality forbids us to believe that our world could not in any circumstances be totally destroyed; that in the event of a nuclear war we or some of us or some others must inevitably survive; that the responsibility for preventing such a war is anybody's but ours; that if we fail in that responsibility God would save us from the inevitable consequences. The nuclear reality is already – quite apart from its possible consummation in future – the harshest judgment on our human world. It confronts us already with the hell of a total extinction that we will have brought upon ourselves. It calls in question every human purpose by threatening an end to all purposes and casting over every human achievement the shadow of the greatest possible failure. It takes away every consolation of the future, every hope vested in our children and their children after them. It robs us of that most natural form of hope, the confidence that there will always be a tomorrow. Under such a judgment, which most of us already feel in our guts if we haven't thought it in our heads, it might seem that we have already abandoned hope and entered the gates of hell.

Yet just because the judgment can already be heard it offers the possibility of hope. This is the paradox at the heart of the prophetic message, only now in the extremity of the nuclear situation it comes to us in an even more radical form. What threatens us so harshly from the future, the end of the world, is itself a source of hope for a new world. It takes with one hand everything we hold dear, but with the other it returns everything to us a hundredfold. It promises to destroy our world and recreate our world at one and the same time. The unravelling of this paradox lies in the simple fact that we are responsible for what happens. If we are annihilated in a nuclear conflagration, that will not be the result of an abstraction like 'world politics', 'technological progress' or 'the course of history'; it will be the result of our own (collectively arrived at) human decisions. More specifically, it will be the outcome of the pursuit of human power and material security which gave us the bombs in the first place. And we shall pursue these policies of power and violence only if we continue to believe, as some of us still foolishly do, that they will secure our peace and prosperity. But it is precisely those beliefs which are called in question by the nuclear threat. Or, to be more emphatic, we should say that the deepest purposes which are leading our nations to construct and deploy these forces of destruction are themselves being undermined by the secret operation of the universal threat that they pose. Human hearts are easily misled into the worship of idols of power and destruction, but when the fear of being destroyed at the hand of those idols also enters their hearts they are likely to lose their confidence. More likely still, they will be disgusted and stricken with remorse. Such feelings may not be made public, but they may find expression in a genuine struggle for an alternative form of security, and perhaps an alternative source of life and meaning. The judgment on our present way of life gives us – including those of us most committed to the idols of nuclear power – a new freedom to choose otherwise.

We are not entitled to say, even in our most despairing moments, that history is moving incxorably to its end. There may be, it is true, as Edward Thompson has argued, a 'logic of exterminism' in the arms race, but there is also in opposition to that and in response to its horrifying outcome a logic of survival in the hearts of human beings. There is reason to hope that human beings throughout the world will be so awakened by the nuclear threat that they will see to it that the logic of survival prevails. But in that hope there is embedded a deeper hope, for the hope of survival in a nuclear age implies that we will learn how to live with one another without resort to violence as the source of security. We will have to learn to trust one another instead, even across the boundaries of nations and power blocs: indeed, we may have to trust one another enough to do without these boundaries altogether – the moral 'have to' is part of the new logic of survival. The age-old hope of the brotherhood and sisterhood of humankind now has a new and politically realistic basis in the knowledge that no other form of human relations can be safe against the nuclear threat. Even with a new form of human relations we shall still not be absolutely safe, since with their freedom and unpredictability humans can always put themselves and others at risk. Human life will continue to be as risky as it always was. But it is possible, and with the new logic of survival it is necessary, that we take collective responsibility for life on earth and, as a first major step, dismantle the whole apparatus of collective death. We should then ensure that we would not be exposed to the risk of human annihilation by mistake.

There are then good grounds for hoping that human life will take this new and dramatic turn, because the implications of not doing so are already penetrating our consciousness with the power of a message from God. There is no ground for believing that human life will, most certainly, develop in this way. It is still possible that we shall fail to respond to this new reality and therefore suffer the inevitable and irreversible consequences. But that is just the point. We are free to choose. It is our responsibility. It is perhaps the most frightening responsibility we humans have had to bear, but it is only in taking on that responsibility, with the courage to accept the implications of failure, that we shall find strong reasons for hoping. It is at least reassuring to know that the immediate source of hope is in the very object of our present despair. The mysterious event on the horizon which is casting a dark shadow of gloom over us is also shedding a light on us, disclosing the inner meanings and possibilities of our existence. It is enabling us to see the futilities of self-centredness and of the idolatry of power, and to see the possibilities of living in mutual trust and care as a profoundly fulfilling mode of life. This is not only to say, as the mystics said, that the light we seek comes out of the darkness we fear, but that with the light there comes a freedom to choose what we most profoundly need, and with that choice there comes an experience of life's meaning.

In this remarkable way we are being liberated by a power beyond ourselves, and beyond even our comprehension. The reality on which our existence ultimately depends is confronting us both in the threat of extinction and also, through that threat, in the creation of a new possibility altogether. It confronts us with a new and decisive either/or: either we commit ourselves unreservedly to the creation of a new world in which people trust and affirm one another, or we continue with the world as it is and help bring it to an end. It is therefore, surprising as it may seem, making us a gift of the life we have always longed for, but it is a gift we must grasp with both hands in order to receive. It is not being foisted on us against our will, in defiance of our freedom and responsibility. On the contrary, it is a gift that enhances our freedom so that in freedom we can now exercise our new responsibility to care for the whole earth.

Hope is based on trust, not on certainty about an inevitable outcome. And what we can trust, in order to be able to hope, is this ultimate power of reality that comes to us out of the darkness of the world situation and arises in us to affirm one another and creation as a whole. It is indeed the God who created our world and now, through us, can recreate it.

7

Prayer in the Belly of the Beast

Terry Tastard SSF

Today there is a pressing need for concerned Christians to develop a spirituality which is consciously related to the nuclear horizon. This project seems hardly to have been tackled. The ethical dimensions of nuclear weapons have been extensively examined; by contrast, little effort seems to have gone into thinking about how the ways in which we pray relate to the nuclear horizon.[1] The development of such a spirituality would have at least two positive effects. It would help remedy a spiritual sickness, namely the fatalism or even despair which characterize nuclear nations. And it would have an important role to play in bringing about a full and informed consciousness of the implications of nuclear weapons.

Spirituality is notoriously difficult to define. Perhaps the most useful definition is Gordon Wakefield's suggestion that spirituality is 'the way in which prayer influences conduct, our behaviour and manner of life, our attitudes to other people.'[2] In using this definition we must, however, avoid the temptation to conceive of prayer as the individual's private relationship with God: prayer takes many public forms, such as liturgy, vigil, singing and dancing.

What nearly all prayer has in common is hope. In the Christian tradition – which is the only one I am qualified to write about – we pray because we are people of hope. Take intercession, for example. It is difficult to give any rationale for intercession, yet many Christians persevere in intercession almost because of a kind of inner compulsion. Underlying intercession is the hope that the world's condition is not immutable, that injustice, for example, can be checked and suffering brought to an end. Alternatively, take the eucharist: those who gather around the altar hope that this shared act of prayer will bring them new strength through sharing in the risen life of Christ. Another example could be the prayer of confession and repentance, which depends on the hope that past patterns of behaviour will not be endlessly determinative for the future.

Hope, then, is an important component of prayer. Yet hope sometimes seems in short supply in precisely those nations which possess nuclear arms. When Lesslie Newbigin returned to Britain after nearly forty years in India, his greatest problem of readjust-ment was moving from the hopefulness of India to the hopelessness of Britain.[3] Even in the most squalid slums of Madras he found a hope in the future which he felt had disappeared in Britain. This is anecdotal evidence, of course; but it fits my own experience of Africa and Central America. Often the people of poor nations with fragile economies have a greater sense of the openness and promise of the future. By contrast, the nations which have the awesome power of nuclear weapons are precisely those which have the greatest sense of despair. I would not argue that the hopelessness found in such countries is entirely due to nuclear arms, but I do believe that this factor is one of the most significant causes. Opinion polls regularly show that a substantial majority of people expect cataclysmic nuclear war in their own lifetime. The resulting dread inevitably takes its toll on people's confidence and energies, particularly where the dread is repressed.[4] Hence the irony that people scrabbling to earn a living in the two-thirds world sometimes exhibit a vitality and a hope that people living in more prosperous countries do not.

In this sense the development of nuclear weapons is a classic case of alienation. Life and energy have drained away from the creators into the object of their creation. Marx's description of this process seems particularly apt:

The worker puts his life into the object, and this means that it no longer belongs to him but to the object . . . the greater this product, the less he is to himself . . . it exists outside him, independent and alien, and becomes a self-sufficient power opposite him.[5]

In this kind of process nuclear weapons assume a life of their own, and in so doing become cause and symbol of human powerlessness. The cult of nuclear weapons accrues power to itself and seems now to develop under its own momentum, beyond human control. We need to develop a spirituality which speaks to this situation. It will need to be a spirituality which will help us expose and confront fear, and one which will encourage us to find a new freedom of action.

Prayer in a nuclear age, if it is to be honest, must help us come to grips with the tendency to evade responsibility for nuclear policies. There is an inherent tendency to ascribe wisdom to people in positions of power. Powerful people generate an image of virtuous omniscience. The decisions they take are presented as the wisest possible ones. Of course, this kind of tendency long predates the development of nuclear weapons, but that development strongly reinforces the tendency. The association of nuclear weapons with national security, plus of course the complexity of nuclear technology itself, combine to generate an atmosphere in which a relieved public is prepared to believe that the few people at the top who are in possession of 'all the facts' are uniquely suited to decide on our behalf. But the honesty which is essential to prayer should not allow us to evade responsibility in this way.

Among Christians aware of such issues, the need is for a spirituality which will help us acknowledge the hopelessness which nuclear weapons create, a spirituality which will also help us recover our freedom to act in this situation. I shall choose two aspects of prayer to help illustrate the possible shape of such a spirituality: meditation; and repentance and lament.

1. *Meditation*

Meditation as I shall use it is a form of prayer in which a person dwells on the images created, the emotions felt or the thoughts that arise in response to various subjects. These could be biblical passages, or ideas or concepts (for example, 'forgiveness', 'the love of God', etc.). Alternatively, meditation can begin with a person's ordinary surroundings, and by relating these to God can increase the awareness of God in everyday life. Meditation can thus take the form of freeing the thoughts or imagination to explore the relationships and interconnectedness of our world. Meditation can be an intellectual exercise or it can be the creation of mental pictures. It can be explicitly religious or it can be practised by people who do not see it in that light.

Put in such terms, meditation sounds inward-looking and passive. Sometimes it has been both those things. Yet meditation can also be a powerful means of predisposing us towards action. In a nuclear age it can both free us and energize us to work for peace. Meditation can do this because it relates to those half-submerged areas of each person's consciousness which strongly influence behaviour. Thanks to psychology, we are more aware of the importance of this area of our consciousness than ever before. We are also afraid of it, because we identify this area as one of sexual fantasy, of primitive longings and ego-centricity. While this is true, it is only part of the picture, because this same area of our personality contains other desires and longings: the desire to give and receive love, to affirm and be affirmed. It is also the area where we find ourselves being moved by ideals which attract us. Anybody tempted to deny this should recall the way that patriotic fervour boiled up from nowhere, as it were, in Britain during the Falklands saga, with consequences which endure to the present day.

Using Ignatian techniques of meditation, several best-selling books on spirituality have been published in recent years which utilize these longings and desires by channelling them into prayer in a way that will dispose a person to act for justice and peace.[6] Such exercises are always open to the objection of flight from reality. Yet the best-selling success of these books seems to have tapped a hitherto hidden demand for a spirituality which will both deepen our relationship to God *and* deepen our commitment to care for the world of which we are part. Moreover, meditation takes place in that area of human creativity where will and action, reason and emotion, all intersect. This is one of the reasons why meditation can empower us to act. Sometimes poetry in the soul can mobilize us in a way that a political manifesto cannot.

The time has come to develop forms of meditation which are related to the challenge of our nuclear horizon. Nuclear (and ecological) problems have led to a stage where we have to find new ways of relating to both God and the world. Thus the United States theologian Sallie McFague says that given these problems, we have to create a new understanding which would help us to see 'the God-world and human-world relationships as open, caring, inclusive, interdependent, changing, mutual and creative'.[7] One example of how meditation can do this would be the work of her fellow-American Joanna Rogers Macy, who believes that the most important contemporary issue is helping people to overcome their sense of powerlessness when confronted with the problems of society. Drawing from different traditions, religious and non-religious, Macy has devised group activities and meditations with a twofold aim, first of getting people to articulate their fears of global destruction, second, of helping them to experience the power to influence the course of events and create an alternative future in which it is life that triumphs.

Using her exercises and some of my own with groups has always produced a positive response. I hesitate to try to convey them. In a co-operative group setting, perhaps with the use of music, they may work well. On the other hand, read privately from the page they may come across as flat or even maudlin. However, here is an extract from one of Joanna Macy's most effective exercises, which she calls 'Envisioning our Descendants'. She invites us first to think of our youngest living descendant, such as our own child, or our nephew/niece, or a baby yet to be born. She goes on:

> Imagine that some time has passed and this person has had a child of his or her own. Picture this new baby. Does it look like you at all?

> Now allow this baby to grow up, to become an adult. Picture the baby he or she brings into the world. Notice the eyes, the chin, the colour of hair. . . . This descendant grows up and, in time, becomes ready to have a child too. The thread of life continues, and another generation, a new baby, is born.

> We're about a century in the future. See this child taking its first steps: watch it mature from infancy to childhood. . . . Perhaps this child lives in a world that is free of the imminent threat of nuclear war. What does the child say to you? Perhaps the child thanks you for the work you did in your lifetime to ensure the world's continuance. Listen to the child for a few minutes . . .

What do you tell your descendant about what it was like for you facing the nuclear threat in the twentieth century?

. . . Now for the next few minutes, let yourself be with the child. Perhaps the two of you continue to talk; perhaps you are together in silence.[8]

One strength of this particular meditation is that it takes seriously the fear of total annihilation, the fear that comes with being the first people on earth with the power to prevent all birth and thus to annihilate not just ourselves but all future generations. But the meditation does not allow this realization to cripple, paralyse, or depress. Instead it uses this honesty about the present and future to unblock our energies, and to work for the future out of love for what that future could contain. I have used an example which does not depend on traditional religious imagery. Exercises are possible which do use such imagery, the eucharist, for example, or the Pauline image of believers as the body of Christ. Meditation approached in this way helps us become participants in social change rather than victims of it.

2. *Repentance and lament*

The prayer of repentance has a long history in the Judaeo-Christian tradition. In its fully developed form it traditionally comprises a review of past life, an expression of contrition for sins, request for divine assistance and the promise of amendment of life. Repentance thus weaves together past, present and future.

There is an acute need for the development of forms of prayer which express repentance for nuclear sins. Wendell Berry notes that

What we are proposing to ourselves and to the world is that we are prepared to die, to the last child, to the last green leaf, in defence of our dearest principles of liberty, charity, and justice. It would normally be expected, I think, that people led to the brink of total annihilation by so high and sober a purpose would be living lives of great austerity, sacrifice, and selfless discipline. That we are not doing so is a fact notorious even among ourselves. Our leaders are not doing so, nor are they calling upon us or preparing us to do so.[9]

We need to develop forms of repentance for private prayer and public liturgy which will remind us of this holocaust which is being proposed in our name. Some such forms of repentance have been developed. For example, each year Christians hold a service of repentance outside the Ministry of Defence in London on Ash Wednesday, during which the walls are marked with ash. The creation of forms of repentance is not limited to Christians, of course; some of the most potent symbols have come from people of other religious traditions or none, such as the festooning of barbed wire fences at nuclear bases with photographs of loved ones, or the spraying of shadows on pavements to remind us of similar ghostly traces left by people vaporized by the bomb at Hiroshima.

It is in these ways that repentance can become part of a spirituality in which we recall sin embedded in society, confess our collusion with it, and seek to change this situation. There needs to be greater awareness of the need for repentance in relation to nuclear policies. As Wendell Berry reminds us, nuclear-armed powers are not exactly in a state of sombre recollection when they propose mutual destruction; indeed, such destruction could take place through human or mechanical error. Repentance is needed to remind us and others of the possible consequences of what is being planned in our name. Pilgrimages, litanies, songs, dances and other activities are being developed; we need to increase the number and variety of these participatory forms of prayer into which people can enter.

Some important work has been done here already. For example, the British theologian Janet Morley wrote the following prayer for a march at Upper Heyford USAF on 6 August 1987, commemorating both the Transfiguration of Jesus and the anniversary of the dropping of the bomb at Hiroshima. The march included a prostration at the foot of the cross:

> Christ our only true light,
> before whose bright cloud
> your friends fell to the ground:
> we bow before your cross
> that we may remember in our bodies
> the dead who fell like shadows;

and that we may refuse to be prostrated
before the false brightness
of any other light,
looking to your power alone
for hope of resurrection from the dead.[10]

Here Janet Morley has skilfully woven together the symbols of a much-loved gospel story and the symbols of the tragedy at Hiroshima, in a way that evokes a response of commitment. This sensitivity to past and present is a hallmark of her work, and it can be seen in another example, an as yet unpublished litany called *Improperia for Good Friday*. Here is an extract from this contemporary set of Reproaches:

Holy God, holy and strong, holy and intimate, have mercy on us

O my people, what have I done to you, how have I offended you, answer me.

I brooded over the abyss, with my words I called forth creation; but you have brooded on destruction, and manufactured the means of chaos.

O my people, what have I done to you, how have I offended you, answer me.

I breathed life into your bodies, and carried you tenderly in my arms; but you have armed yourselves for war, breathing out threats of violence.

O my people, what have I done to you, how have I offended you, answer me.

I made the desert blossom before you, I fed you with an open hand: but you have grasped the children's food, and laid waste fertile lands.

O my people, what have I done to you, how have I offended you, answer me.

Holy God, holy and strong, holy and intimate, have mercy on us.

In this litany evocative passages from Genesis, Hosea and elsewhere, together with venerable liturgical material, are woven into a reminder of the urgent issues of today. Morley's work is in this sense truly prophetic, for it is an example of what Walter Brueggemann points out is a characteristic role of the prophet: to reach back into the 'deepest memories of the community' to activate symbols which can contradict the official ideology.[11]

There are other ways in which the official ideology, or in Brueggemann's terms, the 'regnant consciousness' needs to be challenged by repentance. Nuclear societies produce an extraordinary level of denial, both at the official level and at the popular. At the official level we are repeatedly told that nuclear weapons and nuclear power are utterly safe and that accidents are almost impossible. When accidents do happen, we are told that they are of little consequence. At the popular level, we find the same views being put forward by people who work in nuclear industries and who are understandably anxious to protect their jobs at a time of high unemployment.

This process of popular denial is fully described by Grace Mojtabai in her book *Blessed Assurance*, based on her stay in Amarillo, Texas, where the Pantex plant makes 1500 nuclear warheads a year. What she found was a community that evaded its pain, sometimes using the well-known rapturist doctrine to do so, holding that a nuclear holocaust would be preceded by the Second Coming of Christ in which the saved will be swept up to heaven. A puzzled Mojtabai muses that this stress on the Second Coming and on the irredeemability of the world 'strangely negates the "good news" of the gospels and of the First Coming'.[12] This particular doctrine has made little headway in Britain, but we have our own processes of denial. In July 1987 I arranged for a debate to take place in a parish church near a factory in England which assembles nuclear warheads. The debate was to have been between an aeronautical engineer who had resigned from work on nuclear missiles on conscience grounds, and a retired admiral who still believed in the appropriateness of such weapons. At the last minute the arrangement was cancelled by a churchwarden, who wrote that it was not the wish of the Parochial Church Council 'to have our church used for a public debate on a political issue, especially one which has such strong local involvement'. Yet medical statistics have shown the possibility that this area has an abnormally high leukaemia rate.

In this sort of context we need a spirituality in which repentance becomes lament. Repentance could be linked to making visible the people who have already been victims of nuclear policies; the service personnel compelled to be guinea-pigs in nuclear tests, the victims of accidents in nuclear power stations, the Pacific Islanders moved from their ancestral homes to allow for testing and sometimes still suffering from the fall-out. For these and other nuclear sins we need to express contrition, and we need to be aware that it matters not just how we pray but where we pray. The fences of nuclear installations are appropriate places for repentance and lament just as altars are appropriate places for the eucharist. We need to develop lament that will uncover the hidden pain, that will grieve for people and if possible with them. Here again, spirituality becomes prophetic. Public sharing of pain is a way of alerting people to an aspect of reality which is hidden when the pain is hidden. In this sense lament becomes part of a battle for public consciousness, for until the pain is acknowledged the community cannot begin to explore new possibilities for a different way of life. Here again, we glimpse how spirituality in a nuclear age can have a significant role in resisting the controlling ideology. Walter Brueggemann points out that those who lead unjust societies have a considerable investment in wanting their countries to be seen as both efficient and permanent.[13] Efficient, because this promotes the belief that the system gives people what they want. Permanent, because those in charge do not want any exploration of alternative orderings of society. A spirituality of repentance which exposes hurt in the form of lament calls into question both the efficiency and the permanency of nuclear arms and power. To seek to do this in our nuclear context is to put into effect Brueggemann's observation that 'Bringing hurt to public expression is an important first step in the dismantling criticism that permits a new reality . . . to emerge.'[14]

I hope that I have shown how, in a nuclear age, an appropriate spirituality can be developed which builds upon such elements as meditation and repentance/lament. I am aware, however, that spirituality still has connotations to many people of escape, or of an individualistic piety which ignores the needs and crises of society.

Two observations could be made about this. I would begin by pointing out that Christians who are active in social issues tend to come from the liberal or radical wings of the churches. It is a perennial temptation of liberalism or radicalism to rely on the head at the expense of the heart. This can restrict the appeal of their message; it can also mean that they deprive themselves of resources for the struggle. At its best spirituality seeks to integrate both prayer and action, head and heart.

Secondly, all spirituality has a social impact, even an individualist piety. As Gregory Baum puts it,

> Spirituality is not simply a hidden reality. It takes place in the heart, and in this sense it remains invisible to others; at the same time, interiority in any of its forms translates itself into a personal stance towards society and other people, and in this sense becomes socially visible.[15]

In other words, spirituality can help people engage with society or it can distance them from it; it can give them the energy to respond to urgent issues, or the means of evading them. Spirituality is never neutral – which underlines the urgency of building a spirituality against the nuclear horizon.

8

Affirming all our Humanity[1]

Donald Evans

Christianity has not yet become a genuinely humane and incarnational religion. The embodiment of God which Jesus initiated has not been fulfilled in the humanity of Christians. Christian theology has encouraged us to separate far too much of that humanity from the transforming power of the Holy Spirit. One of the results of this constriction has been that in general we have promoted war more than we have promoted peace.

Today, when the extinction of all life on this planet in a nuclear catastrophe is a real possibility, there is a special urgency for Christians to re-examine the beliefs which have shaped our thought and action, beliefs which usually have not effectively inhibited our tendencies to foster institutionalized conflict. Radical revisions may be required.

Some theologians will immediately retort that Christianity has not been tried and found wanting, but has not been tried. That is, the only revision that is needed is not in Christian beliefs, but in Christians. There is some truth in this, but not the whole truth. For as we look back over Christian history it is now clear that some of the most saintly Christians legitimized violence and oppression against 'outsiders', whether these were heretics or witches or people of other religions or other cultures. They were corrupted as much by what they believed as by their own personal flaws.

The Christian community has much blood on its hands, much need for repentance. And repentance includes a re-examination of its beliefs. Fortunately, however, there is much *within* Christian theology on which we can draw as we review it in relation to peace.

Part of what is required is a re-emphasis on elements in our tradition which have been ignored or distorted, though we must also explore new implications of that tradition in relation to an evolving understanding of our humanity.

Within Christian theology three basic beliefs need to be re-affirmed. First, being human involves being part of the human community on this planet, sharing in a common origin as the image of God, a common entanglement in evil, and a common destiny at the End of history. Nothing human is fundamentally alien to any one of us. Second, God became human in Jesus so that we also might come to embody God, both individually and communally. We can learn to embody God in ways similar to Jesus, but also in new ways which, though compatible with his incarnation, are not included in it. Third, what it means to be fully human is only gradually being lived and understood by human beings as we learn how to incarnate God with our whole selves. Human existence is historical, and human nature is changing. Only at the End will our humanity be fully transformed and fully disclosed as the revelation of God.

Christians have been most destructive when these beliefs have been suppressed or perverted. Often we have lost our sense of common humanity, treating non-Christians at best as 'strangers' and at worst as enemies. Often we have insisted on belief in Jesus as the only incarnation of God, excluding from salvation anyone who rejects that belief, and even from humane treatment by us. Often we have presumed to know already what human nature is and can be, refusing to learn from other religions or cultures any elements of what it means to be human, any ways to incarnate God.

What Christians need is a theology which sees the whole human community as learning in various ways how to be lived by God in all the dimensions of our humanity, in spite of our common entangle-ment in evil. In this process Christians are empowered by the indwelling Christ, who re-affirms our connection with all of humankind. As Christians we can be open to broaden and deepen our understanding of what it means to be human, so that eventually the whole self can be surrendered into the divine life.

Many dimensions of our humanity need to be included in our understanding and in our lives, but four are specially important in relation to world peace. One dimension may be called the 'global-humanistic'. Human beings need to nurture their sense of connection with humankind as an intimately-interdependent global community. Another dimension may be called the 'inner-ecological'. Human beings need to re-discover their inner resonance with everything in the world of nature, especially their sense of being rooted in planet earth. A third dimension is often called the 'dark side'. Human beings need to uncover the repressed and unowned destructiveness which otherwise we project on to others, who thereby become at best strangers and at worst enemies, regardless of their reality. And a fourth dimension may be called the 'oppressed feminine'. Human beings need to recognize as a major source of institutional violence the radical distortions in human nature produced by millennia of male domination.

The four perspectives on human nature which I am advocating are not the only ones relevant to peace-making. Moreover, they do not by themselves answer crucially urgent questions concerning what military and political strategies will best promote peace, or concerning the moral dilemmas which all proposed strategies seem to create. But long-range issues concerning basic perspectives are also important, and should not be neglected. If we are to learn how to live through the twenty-first century with our knowledge of how to build the Bomb, we obviously need to have some perspectives which reduce our reliance on institutionalized conflict. So I am proposing four such perspectives for serious consideration. In each case Christians are challenged to revise our belief-structures, but in ways which broaden and deepen our understanding of their incarnational essence.

A *global-humanistic* perspective is initially difficult for many Christians, for various reasons. One obstacle is the liberal individualism which Protestantism has spawned in Western culture generally. How can I have any sense of being inherently and intimately involved, for good and ill, with all of humankind if I am essentially an atomic individual? Since a liberal's connections with others depend entirely on his free choice to enter into social contracts, the best an altruistic liberal can do is to 'opt for humanity', creating a connection rather than experiencing it, assuming responsibility rather than acknowledging it. And since each liberal consciousness is allegedly sealed off from any direct influence by other private consciousnesses, it seems that we can only affect each other through material media. In contrast with this, a global sense of connection with humankind includes an awareness that we influence each other not only in our institutional power-structures and in the public events which the media report but also on a psychic and spiritual plane. Long before modern communications arose to intensify our human togetherness, we lived in a global village, influencing each other around the planet towards hope or despair, trust or terror, compassion or rage, peacefulness or violence.

Obviously social-contract liberalism is incompatible with traditional Roman Catholic and Orthodox teachings concerning community, and private-consciousness liberalism is incompatible with much in the spirituality of pre-Enlightenment Christendom. But criticisms of liberalism based on appeals to earlier Christian doctrines are not adequate if Christian theology is to nurture a sense of world-wide human community. The hurdle for many Christians is still their restriction of community to *Christian* community, so that non-Christians are, at best, 'strangers whom Christ loves'. Instead of having a sense that nothing human is alien to me and that we human beings are all in this thing together, many Christians are still influenced by the exclusivism of most traditional theology. If there is no salvation outside the church, or outside correct beliefs concerning Jesus, non-Christians are aliens. If one's primary sense of identity is Christian rather than human, then even if Christian beliefs are held by post-liberals in a relativistic true-for-us way (which implies that non-Christians may have true-for-*them* beliefs), there is still no sense of participating in a common humanity. This humanity has not yet completely evolved, but it already transcends many of the differences which divide us, and it includes much that unites us.

Fortunately there are new global rituals, initiated by Christians or welcomed by Christians, which are challenging Christian exclusivism and nurturing a sense of our common humanity. Pope John Paul initiated a 'meeting together to pray' in Assisi, drawing together representatives of diverse religious traditions who are united by a common concern for peace. This was not a 'meeting to pray together' he explained, for no common prayer was proposed or used; but each person can be 'present' while others pray. Such a procedure, while theoretically still compatible with Christian exclusivism, implies some legitimacy in non-Christian prayer, so he was criticized by ultra-conservatives.

The new challenge for Christians is to broaden our sense of spiritual community, becoming fully ecumenical not only concerning whom we pray *for* but also concerning whom we pray *with*. If humankind can begin to pray together we can begin to learn how to live together, finding new and creative ways to reduce the likelihood that we will all die together in the mutual mass murder of a nuclear war. But how can we pray together with integrity, when we differ so much in beliefs? These differences should not be ignored in a desperate intellectual search for a least-common-denominator unity in doctrine or a prayer-wording which everyone can tolerate.

The best way to begin to pray and meditate together is in *silence*. Words are not enough. In silence we can sense that we are not separate from anyone, and so we can dare to hope for peace. In silence we can let go, for a short time, of our desperate clinging to the convictions which separate and divide us, letting these recede to the background of consciousness. After the silence, we return to deal with the same differences, but in a different spiritual climate.

On the third Tuesday of September each year the United Nations Assembly invites all humankind to join in a minute of silence on the International Day of Peace. Such a global ritual is open in principle to every human being on earth, of every faith and of no faith. In 1986 millions of people participated around the world.

A world-wide minute of silence for peace expresses a new level of awareness which is emerging in the consciousness of humankind. Not so long ago, only a few saints and mystics were personally aware of being deeply connected with all other human beings, for good and ill. In the 1980s, however, there have been many symbolic public events which have both evoked and expressed such an awareness of human solidarity, though the awareness is as yet mostly rudimentary. In July 1985, Live-Aid focussed the caring of millions of people on world hunger. In May, 1986, five million people joined Hands Across America, spurred by secular celebrities and Billy Graham. Though this event was not planetary in focus or scope, it was similar in its invitation to set aside differences to join in a symbolic public event expressing a common concern. In June 1986, rock stars joined with Amnesty International to raise consciousness concerning the plight of political prisoners around the world.

We are witnessing a dramatic shift in human consciousness. It arises partly from new contact between people around the world through TV and radio, partly from a new awareness of our economic and political interdependence, and partly from a new sense of shared vulnerability to nuclear holocaust and ecological disaster. But there is also a spiritual dimension to this movement towards human community, a heart-felt sense of connection and kinship, an experience of our common humanity.

The global rituals which nurture and express this change in human self-understanding are not a substitute for concrete policies to reduce the likelihood of war. To see them as a substitute is to succumb to a disembodied spirituality, a romantic sentimentalism. But if the overall spiritual climate within which policies are considered and implemented is mostly negative, it is unrealistic to expect much progress towards peace. Clever strategizing and righteous protesting are necessary, but by themselves they are usually futile.

Christians should welcome the new global rituals not only because they help to improve the spiritual climate around the world and thereby facilitate practical peace-making but also because they are first steps towards a global humanism, towards the embodiment of God in all humankind. As Father Zosima says in *The Brothers Karamazov*, 'Every one of us is answerable for everyone else . . . if we knew this, we would at once have heaven on earth . . . Until that day we must keep the hope alive'.

We also need an *inner-ecological* perspective to extend our self-understanding beyond humankind to include the whole of nature. Our interdependence with nature has become evident to some scientists, in spite of the basic scientific perspective which detaches us from nature as its observers and manipulators. And a new ecologically-oriented science is helping to remedy our ravages of nature by inventing new technology. But this is inadequate as an inhibitor of further ravages and as a basis for understanding what it means to be a human animal-vegetable-mineral.

What is required is an *inner* ecological perspective, that is, an awareness of nature within oneself, an experiential understanding of embodiment. In response to this requirement Christianity is ambivalent. On the one hand, as the religion of incarnation, of Word becoming flesh, it has the strongest possible basis for exploring every dimension of embodiment so that the whole self may be lived by God rather than only the intellectual self or the spiritual self or the communal self. On the other hand, however, Christianity has inherited from its Jewish origins an abhorrence of anything that seems to resemble nature-worship, and this has deterred Christians from exploring 'primitive' religious paths and thereby learning how it feels to resonate with nature inside oneself: celebrating inner connections with earth and moon and sun and stars, experiencing within oneself the vibrating energies of a bear, a lotus or a crystal, regressing back through one's evolutionary history to one's elemental origins, integrating sexual passion into the whole of life.

Christians must realize that a grateful and reverent acknowledgment of our embodiment within nature is not nature-worship. Rather, it is a rediscovery of a dimension of our humanity which can then be surrendered into the divine life. It is true that without such surrender we are involved in idolatrous worship of the non-ultimate, but this danger arises for every aspect of human life, not solely our embodiment within nature. All our technologies and ideologies and theologies become idolatrous in so far as they are not surrendered into the divine life. Fear of idolatry has been too closely identified by Christians with fear of nature as such. Nature has been the alien 'other' and even the enemy. The alternative to this is not a sentimental view of nature as friend, which still implies that nature is an 'other'. The alternative is a sense that nature is part of us and we are part of nature, that we are not separate. It is true that we are not identical with nature, but every dimension of our humanity is pervasively influenced by our embodiment within nature, which both enriches and limits our existence. To fear nature is to fear a substantial part of what makes us human.

Recently the United Church of Canada formally and publicly apologized to native Canadians for being destructive towards their religion. This act of communal repentance was important, but the next step is to learn from native traditions – and from traditions of feminine spirituality which have survived centuries of Christian persecution – how to re-experience our non-separation from nature.

What has all this to do with peace? A great deal. First, it is obvious that people with a strong inner-ecological conscience have a concern for planet earth which reinforces their concern for humankind: a double concern which issues in action to prevent a nuclear catastrophe which could destroy *all* life. In addition, an inner-ecological perspective helps us to understand better what peace actually is. Peace is not only the absence of institutionalized violence, though it includes this. Peace is, more fundamentally, a discernible spiritual 'climate' or 'mood' or 'vibration' which pervades not only humankind but also nature. Its opposite is a pervasive disharmony and disconnection. Planet earth, with all its human and non-human inhabitants, is like an organism. Its current disharmony and disconnection is a sickness which is experienced as such by people who have an inner-ecological awareness. The earth needs healing if there is to be peace. This healing comes through environmentalist activism but it also comes from rituals of healing for the earth such as those observed by native Canadians. Such rituals should not be dismissed as mere superstitious magic. They express a reality which most Christians are not able to discern. We Christians typically pray to God for nature as if we were not part of nature. In such prayer we are rebelling against the very embodiment into which God creates and calls us.

A ritual of healing for the earth need not be an idolatrous substitute for prayer to God. It can be the embodied mode for such intercession. Together with native people we can humbly acknowledge and celebrate our finitude. We offer up to God both ourselves in nature and nature in us. A friend of mine once had a vision in which a shaman appeared, wearing a strange and frightening mask, challenging him not to flee. Then the shaman removed the mask, revealing the face of Christ, who said, 'Before you can truly know me as Christ you must know me as shaman'. This is a message, I believe, for all disembodied Christians, whether our flight from nature is expressed in doctrinal intellectualism or born-again spiritualism or moralistic activism.

Repression of our nature-self is similar to expression of our '*dark side*', which is the third dimension to be emphasized in relation to peace. Primitive paranoia is the simplest manifestation of the dark side: I repress my own murderous rage, pretending to myself that I am all niceness and virtue; I project this urge to kill on to other persons or other nations; then I fear them because it seems clear to me that they want to kill me. Individual paranoia easily becomes mass paranoia, cultivated by the state to justify its own power by pointing to Them as a threat to Us. This has been specially pervasive and powerful during war-time, when we are taught to see only the dehumanized face of the enemy so that our atrocities can seem to be justified. If we demonize or degrade Them sufficiently, even a nuclear slaughter can seem appropriate.

One of the great benefits of deep psychotherapy is the sombre realization that nothing human is alien to me, including the most destructive impulses of humankind, and that I tend to project on to others whatever I refuse to own within myself, regardless of the extent to which they are actually behaving destructively. This realization does not mean that I become naive about real evil out there. On the contrary, I can then discern it more accurately. The atrocities of Hitler and Stalin have made it clear that some individuals and some institutionalized structures of power can be almost-entirely evil. This is a realistic insight, not a paranoid projection. Where openness to our dark side is crucial is in acknowledging our *own* evil, both potential and actual. Repression of one's own dark side enables people to suppose that almost all of human evil is out there – whether in Moscow or in Washington – and this provides a basic rationale for strategies of mass murder and for ideologies of self-congratulation. We want to feel good about ourselves as a nation, so we project our dark side on to others, thereby also justifying violence in order to protect ourselves; and all this can go on quite independently of any of the realities of the political-military situation. Even if there is a beam rather than a mote in the eye of the other person, the unacknowledged beam (or even the mote) in my own eye will distort my discernment of the other.

In some ways the notion of a dark side is compatible with traditional Christian teaching concerning sin as a universal tendency to deceive ourselves concerning our true motives. There are, nevertheless, two very serious obstacles to an adequate Christian theology of the dark side. First, Christians still tend to ignore the *unconscious* nature of the dark side, and the need to undergo a gradual process of uncovering it and dealing with it. This process may be a modern depth-psychotherapy or it may be closer to the spiritual paths of saints in many religious traditions, but in either case it becomes clear that neither correct beliefs nor conscientious service nor ecstatic spiritual experiences suffice. Indeed, any of these may be used as diversions from facing one's own hidden terror or hatred or anguish. For example, one of the most persuasive preachers on trust in divine providence went into therapy and found that he was unusually paranoid, and that his fervent preaching had been mainly an attempt to conceal this from himself! Since he was inwardly a stranger and an enemy to himself, his world seemed full of strangers and enemies. At best, the idea of God as Friend gave him something to hold on to – better than nothing, but not an authentic faith.

A second obstacle to Christian exploration of the dark side is the fact that Christians still tend to ignore its *human* nature. We tend to demonize it, or at least to reject it in a heavily judgmental way. Typically we try to eliminate rather than to befriend any destructive tendencies which we uncover within ourselves. By 'befriending' I mean accepting the tendencies as human, as distortions of something which can eventually be integrated into the whole self and thereby transformed. Such a befriending only makes sense if a destructive tendency is essentially a distortion of a human tendency which is basically good, a distortion which involves a dis-integration. If, for example, murderous rage arises from frustrated longings for love, then rage which is acknowledged and harmlessly expressed can become a creative force, a positive energy which empowers a person's commitment to love. In such a context Christians can experience divine forgiveness as the transcendent, enabling Presence at work within the process of befriending and integration and transformation by which we come to own the dark side of our humanity and to allow its vital energies to be transmuted into love. Instead of trying to *eradicate* the evil within ourselves, Christians can let God help us to transform it.

In contrast with a view of a sin as a derivative distortion of a good human tendency some fall-redemption theologies see sin as an autonomous evil tendency, not derivative but independent in its energy. The only way to deal with sin is therefore to eradicate it. Such a perspective can lead to a total rejection of the dark side. And this total rejection often leads to total repression, for unconscious passions tend to remain repressed if they have been rejected in advance. To some fall-redemption Christians, who lack a sense of the priority of original blessing over original sin, it seems better not to open Pandora's box at all than to have to deal directly with all the dreadful demons which lie within. Meanwhile the repressed passions, intensified in their disintegrating power as if in a pressure-cooker, leak out wherever they can in unacknowledged ways. Thus some traditional Christians become very dangerous people. Having rejected so much of themselves, they reject much of humankind, and they spread their contagious hate and fear unconsciously wherever they go, though outwardly their image is sweetness and light.

The problem of the repressed dark side is not confined to Christians, though it is arguable that some elements in Christian theology have helped to create the problem. All human beings repress their dark side to some extent. And there will not be peace but war on earth until most human beings have taken responsibility for most of their dark side. This is the first century in which such a change could realistically seem to be even a remote possibility. Millions of people are at least beginning the arduous process which is required.

Wherever a newly-acknowledged cause of conflict begins to be dealt with we have reason to hope, even if the new insight makes us realize how far we are from peace on earth. This is specially obvious in the case of the fourth and final perspective which I propose. During the last few decades the partly-successful feminist challenge to the systematic oppression of women by men has made it possible, for the first time in human history, to envisage an eventual reconciliation between the sexes based on a genuine equality of power. At the same time it has become obvious to some of us that the most fundamental cause of institutionalized violence in the world is the unresolved conflict between the sexes and the

97

distortions of humanity which this conflict has produced. So we have a new hope: there could be peace on earth if there were peace between man and women. And the new hope is sobering: there will not be peace on earth until this happens – and will this happen in time?

The dimension of human nature which Christians and others need to acknowledge is the '*oppressed feminine*'. The most obvious example of this is the institutionalized injustice which has denied women equal rights and opportunities alongside men. The structures of power in society have been in the hands of men. The prevailing ideologies, whether religious or secular, have legitimized the subordination of women and the constriction of their lives. As the pervasive injustice of the patriarchy becomes evident to many women, the suppressed rage and distrust and pain passed down by women through millennia of male domination begins to be acknowledged and expressed. Sometimes, understandably, this legacy is what is most prominent in feminists.

For some feminists, however, there has also been a recovery and discovery of distinctively feminine ways of thinking, feeling, loving, choosing, being spiritual and doing rituals. In the past men have always subordinated these feminine ways and usually suppressed them whenever men have been in charge of society. Yet it is clear that the distinctively feminine ways of being human are, at their best, less likely to encourage institutionalized violence than any prevailing male mode of behaviour, whether this be the macho warrior, the schizoid technocrat planning strategies, the gang of boys fascinated by powerful toys, the alien dominator of nature, or the god-at-the-top.

All these war-prone tendencies in men are linked with their negative attitudes towards women and towards the feminine dimension within themselves. Dorothy Dinnerstein (*The Mermaid and the Minotaur*[2]) has shown, I think, that the tendencies originate in male infancy as alternative strategies for coping with the fear of being overwhelmed and controlled by the dominant woman, Mother. And Dinnerstein's neo-Freudian perspective can be complemented by Jungian insights concerning the repressed feminine component within each male psyche. As a man explores his dark side in these ways and begins to encounter women with less fear, a more peaceable male begins to emerge, with a deeper inner confidence and less need to dominate.

A more radical change in men's self-understanding is needed, however, if men are to be able to meet women without implicitly constricting the sexual-emotional-spiritual energies of women. In my own experience it is not through Freud or Jung that a man begins to discover the distinctively male energies which can eventually complement the energies of women in a genuine and reconciling way. Rather it is initially through a shamanic process, an experience of one's inner links with nature. There are both masculine and feminine energies in the cosmos, and a man can gradually learn to live in steady openness to both of these, thereby beginning to learn how to encounter women in a sexual-emotional-spiritual way which neither threatens them nor feels threatening to him. But this is only a beginning, for if a deeply-reconciling encounter is to take place the man must surrender his whole self, including his shamanic self, into the divine life. And an analogous but different transformation has to occur in women – a change which I do not presume to define!

The basic challenge to Christian theology in all this is not only a recognition of the institutional rights of women but also, even more fundamentally, an openness to a genuinely embodied spirituality which seeks an embodied reconciliation between the sexes. St Francis and St Clare did not reconcile the sexes, making sexual intercourse authentically a sacrament by working through the ancient enmity between Adam and Eve. No one has done this as yet. The task is just beginning, at the end of this century. We do not as yet understand what it means to be human, and especially what it means to be male and female. This will gradually become clear as the rights of women are secured and as a movement towards reconciliation is thereby made possible.

We need to make rapid progress in understanding what it means to be human, expanding our human self-understanding to include all of humanity, all of nature, our dark side and the suppressed feminine. If we do not, this planet may not continue to be inhabited through the twenty-first century. If we do, we will not only be reducing the risk of nuclear catastrophe, we will also be facilitating the embodiment of God in humankind.

Models of God

9

A Nuclear End: Would God ever let it happen?

Brian Russell

1. *The problem for belief in God*

Many Christians think it is inconsistent for someone who believes in God also to believe that there could ever be a nuclear end to life on this planet. They are puzzled and surprised at the suggestion that God's existence could still allow even the possibility of a nuclear end: the moral credibility and the coherence of what we are to believe about God rules out God allowing such a catastrophe. The possibility of a nuclear end, with uncertainty for the future of the human race, seems to question the power and goodness of God.

Such reactions may show that to some degree there is in each of us a measure of folk religion, expressed in the hope that God provides a reassuring continuity and a guarantee to us when we feel our personal future or the future of our planet is in jeopardy. It may also be true that English Christianity has so emphasized the importance of religion providing pastoral comfort that this may hinder us when we try to think out our theology in response to problems faced in the world. Furthermore, Western religious belief may also have an underlying pragmatism, meaning that the existence of God is assumed as a matter of course to have benefits in giving security to life and to the future of the planet.

In the title of this chapter, a nuclear end refers to a nuclear event which would destroy all capacity for life on this planet, including all human life in the universe in so far as this can be known. I shall explore how we can believe in God in ways that face the challenge of the nuclear horizon.

For many Christians, God could not let a nuclear end happen because for them the Bible gives a firm assurance that God is all-powerful and in ultimate control. The writers of this book are aware of the complexity of applying the insights of the Christian Bible and tradition to the present, and especially today because of the new context in which the human race has the capacity to destroy all potential for life. There are occasions in the biblical witness when the people of God had to suffer the consequences of mis-using freedom when God's promptings had not been allowed to shape human choices. For example, the exile in the Old Testament period was not avoided. However, the exile experience became a cradle of new insight into how God makes new and unmerited beginnings. God did so because it is God's nature to create anew and to invite humanity to share in responsibility for creation. The valley of the dry bones in Ezekiel chapter 37 might be a powerful poetic portrait of a planet in which all potential for life had been destroyed. If so, the passage could speak of God establishing new life. The difficulty in applying this insight today is that the passage relates to circumstances in which a group of people had survived exile and could form a nucleus around which God's people could be restored. But a nuclear war or major nuclear accident would not necessarily allow a remnant to survive with any capacity for life, and so the passage loses its force to give hope to us in facing a possible nuclear end. If the passage speaks of God introducing a new form of life after a nuclear end, the problem is that it lessens the urgency for the human race in the present to act responsibly to avoid a nuclear end and to prepare this planet for the kingdom of God.

The challenge of the nuclear horizon for belief in God is that it asks us to reconsider the moral credibility and the coherence of what we believe about God. Two questions need urgent attention: What can it mean to believe in God as loving? What can this imply for how God is in control and for how humanity exercises freedom?

2. *Believing in God as loving*

During and after both world wars significant voices in Christian experience and thought questioned traditional ways of understanding the sovereign control and holiness of God. This was because God could appear aloof and indifferent to the appalling suffering met in the world. God was seen by contrast to be a God who loves and who therefore out of love takes the pain and predicament of those loved into the divine life.[1] God was envisaged as setting aside certain aspects of divine knowledge and control so that God could be seen in the servant figure of Christ as one who was genuinely at risk among us. Christ was open to doubt, to questioning, to the obscurity and mystery of divine purpose, and was not able to call upon powers to change all the circumstances he met. More recently, various theologians have developed this approach to understand God as eternally self-giving.[2]

As eternally loving, God is active in the world, and God also waits and suffers while the human response to God's love is absent or withheld. This implies that, should there ever be a nuclear end, God would experience and be grievously diminished by it. The unchanging nature of God's love need not imply, however, that God is without a capacity to respond to the circumstances we face because of the nuclear horizon. God's love is unchanging because God consistently invites the human race to share responsibility with God in preventing destruction and in seeking the kingdom. God's love is also unchanging because God has an unending capacity to bear costly self-giving and to be grievously diminished, while continuing to offer new possibilities until there can be a new response to God's love.

It is possible to believe that God can influence the life of the world, and be worshipped as holy, without thinking of God as set apart from the world in a self-contained existence. It is because God is a God of love that God creates. As love is a quality that is expressed in relationship if it is to be fulfilled, love therefore seeks to form and deepen relationships with others.

In this regard, God as Trinity may be seen as an eternal source of love in relationship between Father, Son and Spirit, where love is both given and received. But God's love also seeks to create forms of life in which there is some degree of independence as well as a capacity for free response. God's love would be enriched by the free response of human beings, whereas God's love would not be enriched to the same degree by a grudging response or an obedience which God coerced or compelled from us. If divine love is to create in a way consistent with its nature, then human beings must have a degree of freedom and independence. This freedom includes the possibility that human beings will respond to God and return God's love. But if human freedom is to be genuine, then people also have the possibility of acting in ways contrary to God's purposes. God's creating out of love therefore involves God in vulnerability and risk, and this is the unavoidable outcome of God's loving nature.

The consistent expression of God's love will also create circumstances in which human beings have both the potential and also sufficient guidance so that they can make a chosen and free response to God's purposes. Such guidance can be found, through what we discover of God at work in creation and history, through the experience of believers as interpreted in the Bible and Christian tradition, and through our own prayers and experience of God's promptings.

It is, then, because human beings have as a divine gift both freedom and responsibility, that human beings have in time developed the capacity to make a nuclear end. God's love by its very nature cannot make a gift of freedom and then spare humanity from the serious consequences implied in the gift. God's love will ensure that sufficient understanding is available through knowledge and varied forms of revelation for human beings to grasp the implications and consequences of nuclear power.

As loving, God needs a creation of some kind to share in loving and mutual partnership. If God as loving needs relationships in order for love to be fulfilled, then God is less than fully expressed as God if all capacity for life is ended. A loving God could not remain unchanged by the ending of all potential for life on this planet. Rather, God would bear suffering and be diminished because of the annihilation of life. Forms of life that can respond to God are implied by God's loving nature. Any particular planet or form of human race might not have existed, or might have existed in some other radically different form. But God exists by nature as a loving God who is compelled to seek relationships, and so it follows that some form of created life is necessary to belong with God if God's love is to be fulfilled. God without any form of relationships would not be understood as a loving God, and the approach of classical theism explained below needs modifying. This does not mean, of course, that the planet as we presently know it, let alone the individualistic culture of Western Europe, is implied by God's existence as loving. All that is implied is that, were potential for life on the planet ended, then created life in which there is a capacity for free and conscious response to God, would be initiated by God.

God's unchanging love and holiness, which inspire our worship and service, are shown in God's drive to create life anew, however inconceivable in form such life is to us at present with our inevitably limited imagination. God has the moral perfection to initiate new relationships, despite the appalling annihilation caused by a nuclear ending which would also grievously diminish God. God is sovereign in so far as God can bear and absorb infinite pain and loss, without being wholly destroyed by it; and the absoluteness of God's love involves the determination that a nuclear end to life would not exhaust God's will to risk relationships again. God's dependability is shown in an unbreakable will and capacity to bear rejection and to go on offering new beginnings, beginnings that are offered freely because it is God's nature to act from mercy and grace. God acts in this way because God always desires response and commitment, no matter how partial or inadequate is the response. God is like the light that shines in the darkness, and the darkness cannot ever overcome it (John 1.5).

This chapter has begun from a belief that God as loving is creator. It is important to consider how God as loving can also be pictured as saviour. Would God, out of love, rescue us from our mis-use of freedom?

Since God's love means that human beings have a measure of freedom and responsibility in relation to God, it has been remarked that human beings need sufficient guidance so that they can exercise that responsibility effectively. A loving God would provide sufficient guidance. Revelation is one means by which God could be seen to develop in the human race an awareness and will to be a responsible partner. Scripture is a witness to the experience of those who have met and discovered God at first hand. Scripture has been handed on because it is an interpretation of what was found to be revealed by God through meetings and relationships. The interpretation passed on in scripture is shaped partly by the understanding and circumstances of those who responded to God and interpreted what they experienced. This difference in setting between the biblical witnesses and the present may be part of the way in which God's revelation can aid without compelling or over-riding human freedom. For example, the marks of the kingdom of God as taught and demonstrated by Jesus may serve as guides in the use of human freedom, provided they can apply to a new setting in which human beings have the capacity to destroy all life. Jürgen Moltmann believes that there is hope for the human race because God has promised to intervene in the future to bring the kingdom of God. As this future change is already set in motion through Christ's resurrection, it can therefore influence how humanity exercises responsibility in the present to guide the immediate course of history.[3] Moltmann sees the human responsibility as one of preparing for the coming of the kingdom, though the kingdom is solely God's initiative and act. The kingdom involves a new era of history with a quality of life that establishes justice and peace so that the new era is a true expression of God and part of God's life as Trinity.

While Moltmann does not suggest that God over-rules human freedom in bringing the kingdom, the question is raised whether a loving God who could forsee the consequences of human free action annihilating life, would intervene so that either the human action or its consequences were significantly altered. Would an intervention of God that over-ruled human freedom be consistent with God's love? Would an intervention that prevented human beings bearing the consequences and learning from the mis-use of freedom, be loving? Whatever view is taken in relation to an individual's use of freedom (e.g. in drinking and driving and causing a road accident), does the same logic apply to the capacity to destroy all potential for life? There would be no continuing earthly life for human beings in which the lessons could be applied or spiritual and moral growth result.

The fact is that God has not prevented such appalling events as world wars and the Jewish Holocaust. Humanity has had to accept the earthly consequences of such events. Two views are frequently posed as if they are the only two possibilities: *either* that God over-rules human freedom and natural sequences of cause in nature and history through miraculous intervention; *or* that God remains passive and aloof, not intervening at all in the working out of freedom and causation. But it is not a choice between these two extreme views. There is a third possibility that God is active in present circumstances in a non-miraculous way. Each set of circumstances has a variety of possible outcomes, none of which is fixed or determined in advance. God is involved on the inside of life and so initiates creative promptings into this range of options in our daily circumstances. God acts by means of, rather than by over-ruling, the circumstances and the relationships which people form. These divine promptings may introduce entirely new possibilities not previously appreciated by those involved. The divine promptings may mean that an apparently hopeless situation can be drawn towards an outcome that allows something positive to come out of sin and disarray. While there may be no over-ruling of human freedom or natural causes, the event may be altered and trans-figured because divine prompting has been given in and through human actions. Those who have participated in the event have responded to a divine involvement, one that has intervened to guide a situation in one direction rather than another through human co-operation, so that a new beginning has become possible. The emphasis of this belief in divine prompting encourages us to believe that humanity is invited to face and meet the threat to life posed by nuclear power and technology. Human beings can meet God's invitation and can, by co-operating with God's promptings, make sure that we do not face an inevitable nuclear annihilation.

But would not a God who is saviour ensure that human beings used their freedom to avoid a nuclear end? What it means for God to have power and for human beings to have freedom and responsibility requires further exploration.

3. *God's power and human responsibility*

Christian believers have long pondered what it means for God as creator to be sovereign over creation and history. One approach is the belief that God is in control in such a way that the outcome of all events is governed by God because God has fixed or determined the outcome in advance. Some versions of this approach can be found in contemporary Christian thinking about the nuclear threat to life and each version tends to lessen the urgency and vital importance of responsible human action to prevent a nuclear end coming about.

One version of how God controls all events assumes that God, as good and loving, will ensure that no nuclear event can happen to cause such a catastrophe. God has ruled out a nuclear catastrophe from the beginning and would over-rule any possibility. This view therefore allows no scope for genuine human freedom or responsibility. The only way human beings would experience a sense of freedom and responsibility would be if human actions were sufficiently in accord with God's will that God did not need to over-rule. But this sense of freedom and responsibility would be an illusion. It would be rather like inviting your children to assist you in the vegetable garden, and then watching over them and re-doing all their actions that differed from how you yourself would have acted. There is only growth and development for the children in so far as they learn to imitate your own mind and patterns of behaviour. There is no scope for wrong action, or for growth in responsibility as a result of learning from how to survive and how to deal constructively with spoiled opportunities. The children might become perfect copies of you, but they will never develop in moral responsibility or have scope to make their own choices or contribute imaginatively and creatively. This view of our relation to God allows no risk for either God or humanity, and neither we nor God have a capacity to grow as a consequence of a freely offered relationship. Of course, this view would mean that a good and loving God could not allow a nuclear end to life, but it would also mean that human beings could not grow into the fullness of relationship that God desires to have with each of us. God could not be the loving God in whom we have faith and whom we worship.

But another version of how God determines all that happens holds that God could will a nuclear end as an act of judgment and of salvation. Far from protecting us from a nuclear end, this version promises us a nuclear end as God's intention! If the faithful were to be saved from eternal annihilation, then a nuclear end on this view could be eagerly awaited by the faithful. This version gives no scope or encouragement to exercise Christian responsibility to prevent a nuclear end. God is seen as detached, not an involved and loving God. The salvation hoped for is seen as belonging to an existence outside the realm of this world. The sin and fallen-ness of this world seem only to be retrievable by ending the world and this hardly suggests that God is closely involved on the inside of creation as a loving creator.

It is clear that Christian belief requires a delicate balance in how God's control or power is understood to exist alongside the relative freedom and moral responsibility which is given to humanity. Christian tradition does not give sole emphasis to God as set apart and detached from the world. Classical theism held a form of balance between God's sovereignty and human action. God was thought to have an independent basis for existence, rooted solely in the power and capacity of God. God relies on no outside help to be God. In contrast, the world relies on a cause outside of itself for its existence. The world might not have existed at all, or it might have existed in some form other than that in which it came to exist. There is no question of thinking that God might not have existed, or might have existed in some other form. God is as God is, and in principle God exists whether or not there is any kind of created life apart from God. To this extent, a nuclear end to all life would have no repercussions for God continuing to exist in an unaltered and unimpaired way. However, the planet exists because it is characteristic of God's nature that God creates. God may be pictured as a super-abundant source of goodness which is so complete and perfect that, like a fountain, God's nature overflows with loving goodness and causes a created world.[4] The world therefore demonstrates God's nature and contains some patterns of order by which God's good and loving will can be discovered and accepted in faith.

Within this approach, Thomas Aquinas understood that God remains in ultimate control of what happens and that God has fixed in advance the outcomes of events within the world.[5] Human freedom exists to the extent that people can change and put into effect immediate circumstances; but the over-riding purposes of God are worked out through the varying immediate circumstances. It is like a sports match in which we are still playing out the game. The final outcome of the match has already been decided in advance, but the means by which the final outcome will come about depends upon the play and movement of our human choices. We play to win and *we* do not know what the outcome will be! On this approach, God is all-knowing and this means either that God fixes all the outcomes in advance or that God sees in advance how we will use our freedom and therefore knows the outcome. But either way God can decide in advance how to use and shape all human choices and decisions, and how to weave them towards the final outcomes that are decided in God's all-powerful will.

On this approach, it is possible for some partial destruction by nuclear acts to have been foreseen by God and allowed, provided that the destruction is within God's overall plan and is woven towards the achievement of a higher moral good or purpose. Evil is not denied, but evil is not seen as ultimately resistant to serving God's perfect will. A nuclear end could only be consistent with God's goodness if it were the means by which God gathered everything together for its fulfilment in an after-life. However, it is exceedingly difficult to believe how the destruction of all potential for life on the planet can be morally consistent with God's plan fixed in advance. Since the damage after a nuclear event extends far outside the immediate area, it is increasingly difficult to believe that any partial nuclear annihilation could avoid having in the long-run consequences for all life on the planet.

Classical theism holds that both the world and the revelation given in scripture provide truths about God. This allows human beings to learn how to serve God and how to use their relative freedom in accordance with God's will. Human beings have the potential to be in the image and likeness of God, and so have the possibility of avoiding a nuclear catastrophe, if this is God's will. Certainly, the classical view of God can inspire devotion and worship due to God's perfection and power. But, in contrast to the earlier defence of belief in God as loving, the classical view lacks the strength of the love of God entering into a relationship with created life which implies a vulnerability and risk on both sides.

Christian beliefs which emphasize the sovereignty and control of God have been explored, and found to have a less convincing account of God's loving relationship with created life than that suggested earlier in this chapter. It is also vital to explore the possibility that human beings have absolute freedom and responsibility. Such a view would believe in God as wholly present and involved in all of life and in the depths of the individual's experience. This is in direct contrast to those views of God which believe God to exist in a way that is detached or separate from the world.

British Christianity, especially since the 1960s, has often assumed that God is wholly involved in the midst of daily life. Emphasis upon God as wholly involved or dwelling within the world has the general strength that human responsibility is maximized because human beings are partners with God in the work of carrying forward creation and history. God would rely utterly on human response and co-operation, and God's purposes would be hindered or thwarted if this response was lacking. This partnership would involve genuine risk for God and both God and human-kind would have to bear the consequences of mis-used freedom. The risk for God is so precarious that God's existence may itself be in jeopardy. The destruction of all life on the planet might also mean the death of God if God were to exist solely within the domain of this planet.

The moral value of emphasizing the partnership between humanity and God is that humanity cannot evade its responsibility or draw back into a dependent relation to God. God cannot rescue us from our mis-used freedom. All we need has been given by God through Christ, who demonstrates how to co-operate with God and aids us to order the life of the world so that the nuclear threat is avoided. But what if humanity seeks or needs some additional checks and limits upon human freedom and responsibility? Is there no way in which human decisions or mistakes over nuclear power could be reduced or even overcome? Is there any scope for God's help in restoring lost or spoiled opportunities? Can humanity in fact meet such unlimited responsibilities as those entailed in having the capability to destroy all potential for life on this planet?

The emphasis upon God as wholly involved in the world can lack any scope for God's existence beyond and eternal in relation to the world. This danger is especially marked in the account of Christian belief given by Don Cupitt.[6] The attraction of Cupitt's position fits with some tendencies in British Christianity to see religious belief as a choice of the individual to guide their personal experience and inner life. While Cupitt does not believe that there is a 'God' available to help in a manner external to any individual, he does believe that there are rich traditions of religious belief and behaviour, of which Christianity is a fruitful example. Cupitt sees the individual as having freedom and responsibility to control their own existence by living out wholeheartedly the religious belief they choose. For example, they might choose to follow the selfless love of Christ, and see in him the possibility of discovering new meaning through surrendering oneself as he did in the cross and the resurrection. But Cupitt's account emphasizes how the individual can find depth of meaning, or true selfhood and identity. The inner life of the individual seems to be split off from concern about the state of the world and of society outside the individual. Personal responsibility seems to be split off from a shared responsibility that a society or nation has with regard to the future of the planet. These tendencies may help to illustrate how in Western belief and behaviour human beings have found such difficulty in taking shared human and Christian responsibility for a future under nuclear threat.

While human freedom will always be relative and limited, it is vital to re-discover the capability to be responsible and to work for shared and corporate responsibility within and between societies and nations, if the nuclear threat is to be avoided. Cupitt's account leaves possible that humanity may bring a nuclear end, and this end would also remove the notion of 'God'. There is no scope for God to bring aid and influence upon humanity, other than through the radical freedom and self-sufficiency of individuals. The nuclear horizon vividly exposes this limitation.

The search for salvation for those of us who face the nuclear horizon involves believing both in God's reality as an influence upon us and also in the inescapable responsibility given to the human race.

4. *Searching for salvation on the nuclear horizon*

The biblical prophetic traditions picture God acting through historical events to bring both judgment and salvation. The warnings of future disaster made by the prophets are intended to motivate God's people to act responsibly in co-operation with God so that the disaster can be avoided. Knowing the risks of a nuclear end, the human race already stands under judgment. Human beings judge themselves by their response to the opportunities for action which are found. Clearly a nuclear end can be seen as humanity's own judgment upon itself. But if God acts by means of freely made human choices, can a nuclear end also be seen as God's judgment upon us?

This essay has set out the belief that God is consistent in loving and that God would not therefore intervene specifically through human action to bring a nuclear end as a mark of judgment. Individuals or groups may experience disasters as if judgments upon them, but this is different from claiming that God causes disasters in order to judge. Human beings exist in a complex inter-weaving of relationships, and the sum effect of corporate behaviour far exceeds the contribution of one individual or group. This was poignantly shown during the official enquiry into the Zeebrugge ferry disaster. It seemed that a whole system of working practices on ship and on land had grown up over many years, in which a collective web of behaviour was fraught with risk. The disaster might have been a corporately self-inflicted judgment in which individual employees took part, but not a specific divine judgment. The moral character of God would, on this view of God as loving, rule out God's willing the death of innocent victims. But God bears and receives into the divine life the pain and grief of all those lives unfulfilled and of all those bereaved. The same would be true if a nuclear act ended life on this planet.

The nuclear horizon has created a new context in which to understand our Christian belief because of the threat to all potential for life. In searching for salvation on the nuclear horizon, the priority must be the Christian responsibility through prayer and action to prevent a nuclear end. But believing in God as loving in a consistent way may not change specifically how salvation is received from God on the nuclear horizon compared to other horizons. For example, the resurrection of Christ might provide a powerful illustration of God's capacity to restore existence, including material existence. The resurrection of Christ might point to how God can receive potential from that which is destroyed, and how

God can introduce the potential into a new form of existence. The resurrected Christ has an appropriate bodily form for a new sphere of existence. Whether the newly formed body is the changed earthly body, and how the two bodies are precisely linked, is not significant to this point. The resurrection may demonstrate the creative and saving purposes of God which cannot be finally defeated or thwarted. Confronted with a nuclear ending of life, God would create a new sphere of life, which was appropriately material for its purpose, and in which God's creative and saving purpose would continue to embody consistently God's love.

The New Testament writings also teach that the resurrection illustrates an action of God that can happen in each and every present moment, not just at a personal death or a nuclear end. It is through the response made by each generation that God's gift of saving presence is made effective in the church and in the world. No matter how God is seen to act after a nuclear ending to life, this must not lessen either God's commitment to the present planet or human responsibility for seeking to prepare for God's gift of the kingdom in our present world. The kingdom is approached whenever the world is helped to measure more nearly to God's purposes through the response and co-operation of human beings. This includes taking responsibility for continuing to draw back from nuclear confrontation and for seeking safer ways to use nuclear power for energy and social needs.

It is this world that has been the partner in God's nurturing love through the ages, and hope for personal survival after death or hope that God will create anew after a nuclear end, cannot lessen our responsibility in this world. We must search anew to know what God asks of us that salvation can be found against the nuclear horizon.

10

Theodicy and the God of Hiroshima

Elisabeth Holditch

This essay proposes that a new understanding of God's relationship to the world is the true challenge of the nuclear age. If the traditional metaphysical attributes of God's immutability, omniscience and impassibility are to be accepted they cannot account for the existence of evil, and require the explanation of mystery and eternal life. If the necessity of suffering demands an eternal purpose for its explanation can the thesis that a refusal to tolerate affliction would entail an entirely different concept of God be maintained? The need for change in our understanding of the nature of God in the nuclear age will be discussed. The idea that evil exists in the world as a kind of 'substance' incorporated in the structure of human existence and justified theologically by the concept of original sin will be examined. K. Surin states this is 'an epoch in which it is no longer possible for us to address ourselves legitimately to the problem of evil'.

The notion that natural catastrophes, the Jewish Holocaust and nuclear annihilation are manifestations of God's wrath, is inconsistent with Christian faith in a compassionate God. The theodicist is faced in the nuclear age with the incongruence between faith in a God of love and compassion and an unprecedented degree of evil in the world. At no other time has the need for a meaningful theodicy been so urgent within the Christian tradition. F. Sontag posits a demonic side to God because too much evil exists for it to be beneficial to human beings; whereas the plea of Yung Lee is for an empathetic God who suffers with us. K. Surin evaluates the historical development of theodicy until its dilution after the

Enlightenment into anthropodicy or 'secular' theodicy, that had to explain evil in the world without God's intention or justification. By the time of Hiroshima theodicy was 'long since dead'. The problem of evil is no longer a theoretical discourse but is now vigorously focussed upon real evil perpetrated by humankind as an historical fact. 'A theodicy is not worth heeding if it does not allow the screams of our society to be heard'.[1] If theodicy is to be heard in the nuclear age it must affirm the divine purpose of creation and its fulfilment through the conquest of evil. The crisis of the nuclear age has to be viewed in a wider context than threat and destruction, awesome though these are. We are compelled to realize that humankind is on the verge of a better understanding of mutual vulnerability beyond nationalistic, cultural and religious barriers. It may be questioned whether this changed world view is reflected in theodicy.

Since the events of Auschwitz and Hiroshima theological study has found it impossible to make sense of evil in the world. There may be a distinction in kind between the systematic annihilation of victims by obsessive individuals trained to do so, and the release of an 'experimental' bomb many consequences of which were unknown. Modern technology has ensnared humankind in a new level of evil which has been termed 'permitted evil'. Intentional evil is manifested in the actions of men and women in particular historical and social circumstances which may condone it. 'Permitted evil' occurs as an offshoot of technological advance, such as the Chernobyl disaster.

Theodicy attempts to equate the belief in a beneficent God with the realities of evil and suffering in the world of God's making. In the analysis of F. Sontag the old ideas of God are destroyed because no explanation for evil can be derived from his former moral and metaphysical attributes. The question for theodicy is whether an ultimately good outcome for human endeavour can be achieved unless we revise our beliefs about God and his relationship to the world. Humanity is cowed by its own technology, by over-specialization and the pursuit of supposed 'goods' which ultimately cause affliction and degradation.

There seems to be a cut-off point in consciousness which cannot accept responsibility for human suffering brought about by imper-sonal and mechanistic agencies operating beyond the boundaries of personal intention. Depersonalizing bureaucratic processes are an example of the operation of impersonal evil; this evil is permitted because it cannot be reduced to the intention of particular persons. One may ask whether it is inevitable that human affliction should mount to ever more horrific and self-destructive levels, reaching the point of annihilation, or can it be transformed into a new understanding of human solidarity? As our religious optimism breaks down when confronted by incomprehensible 'permitted evil' we are compelled to look at these events in a different way. The advent of nuclear energy can be viewed in the perspective of a new epoch in the history of creation. Although the events of Hiroshima and Nagasaki were the consequence of Western scientific research, and were almost certainly experimental in terms of their consequences, theological discussion has failed to address this supreme apogee of evil perpetrated by human beings against their own species and habitat. The Jewish Holocaust has become the yardstick of theodicy, perhaps because it can be measured in individual terms, whereas the intimidating reality of nuclear reactions seems to be faceless and forcing a crisis beyond control.

1. *Permitted evil*

In modern times we are confronted with a qualitatively different kind of evil. The difference lies in two sinister characteristics; (1) it is not the direct intention of a moral agent but has a supra-intentional aspect and (2) it arises from apathy to global affliction resulting from technological advance. At a certain point of development the objective seems clear and the intention is specific, but there after supra-intentional ramifications develop. Nowadays it cannot be adequate to define 'natural' evil as that done by 'non-moral' agents without making a regressive analysis of the actual causes. The crux of evil is the intention that exists prior to the apparent cause. Cruelty and the degradation of persons which are integral to the conduct of war are instances of intentional moral evil. The contingencies of war not only permit specific cruelty but provide the occasion to train human beings to perform evil which is not intrinsic to them as persons. Perfectly normal people can be trained to inflict pain and to enjoy the practice of torture; indeed the abnegation of personal integrity is one of the most formidable evils of war.

119

Psychological tests conducted by S. Milgram[2] in the post war years indicated that the tendency to obey authority is stronger than compassion for fellow humans beings. When obedience is prized as a moral good beyond personal integrity then intentional evil, divorced from moral responsibility, is unbounded, unless human beings recognize their actions as *sub specie aeternitatis*. In one-to-one relationships of cruelty, evil and suffering are obvious, but we are unable to project this awareness on to the evaluation of nuclear warfare. Writers on the experiences of war and of the Holocaust are ready to point to human transcendence of evil, which seems miraculously to occur in circumstances of affliction. But when we encounter new levels of 'permitted evil' on the scale of nuclear war, the equation between suffering and beneficial outcome is no longer apparent. It is evident that the exploitation of world resources and the depersonalizing of modern people creates a spiral of 'permitted evil'. While condoning preposterous levels of 'permitted evil' – for other creatures – humankind cannot be said to be acting responsibly in relation to God. There appears to be a cognitive inability to interpret affliction as evil, because of its global dimensions. As the technological capacity to inflict mass destruction, impoverishment and exile on other nations increases, tolerance of 'permitted evil' becomes rationalized and normative.

2. *Apathy and affliction*

The lack of coherence in Christian theodicy which fails to resolve the problem of evil, has led to the view of suffering as a necessary and formative experience in human life. If this understanding of evil is accepted it is seen as both instrumental and an aspect of God's permissive will to bring about greater good. Edward Schillebeeckx, however, considers theological speculation about God's permissive will to be the 'dead end of human thinking when it is confronted with the incomprehensible history of human suffering'.[3] The permitted evil of modern war creates vast numbers of refugees, torture victims and prisoners of conscience suffering meaningless affliction.

If Christian theodicy cannot provide an explanation for evil, can we expect it to provide a solution to the vulnerability of human existence under the threat that endangers the life of the planet? The present situation requires a changed view of suffering, supported by a different understanding of God's involvement in the world. We must ask what it is that enables us to tolerate increasing levels of affliction on other human beings. The affliction that humankind imposes on others through permitted evil is a separate category from the redemptive suffering central to Christian faith. There is no evidence in the modern world that escalating violence is within the capacity of humankind to overcome without a change in apathy towards human affliction. Responsibility cannot be projected on to a transcendent and perplexing deity but must be placed squarely within the intentional reciprocity of human solidarity.

The explanation for the toleration of affliction seems to be twofold: apathy arises from the early understanding of the impassibility of God, and confusion with the redemptive power of endurance. D. Soelle's hypothesis is that suffering belongs to the world while God is beyond its reach, so Christianity has become 'a stranger to pain'. Soelle claims that 'When a being who is free from suffering is worshipped as God, then it is possible to train onself in patience, endurance, imperturbability and aloofness from suffering'.[4] Post-Christian apathy views suffering as fate and Soelle considers that the idea of fate and human apathy are related. This is the apathy that concedes to the nuclear threat; it is the apathy to affliction epitomized in the events of Hiroshima and Nagasaki when 'people saw, but did not see, heard, but did not hear' (Isa. 6.9).

Schillebeeckx ascribes the Christian 'misunderstanding' of suffering to a process which has detached the death of Jesus from its historical circumstances. Vicarious suffering, through and for others, exemplified in Christ, has given unmerited suffering a unique significance and made it a 'separate ingredient' in the reconciliation of humankind to God. Martyrdom became personal and redemptive and this change of value created a theology of suffering, which has tended to justify its infliction on others. Thus a theology of suffering accounts for toleration of global affliction because it is based on the belief in the redemptive power of personal endurance. Can a connnection be found between Christian faith in redemptive suffering and the problem of 'permitted evil'?

3. *The God of Hiroshima*

A theodicy that starts from the realities of evil and suffering in the world cannot avoid making a re-evaluation of the traditional moral and metaphysical attributes of God. The question needs to be asked whether the analogy of a personal God, whom we endow with our own moral norms and logical limitations, can have the attributes usually assigned to God. The belief in a God who acts in history and has the power to control events is central to Christian theism but if God exists in an immutable and infinite reality can it be believed that he could influence natural and moral events in this finite and changing world?

We are concerned in this discussion with the indiscriminate destruction and affliction caused by modern warfare, intensified by thermo-nuclear capability. If human affliction is indiscriminate and unjustified, as epitomized in the story of Job, can we expect to find explanations in the nature of God? A theodicy that relies upon the philosophical concept of God as immutable, impassible, perfect and transcendent cannot address the problem of evil except as an inscrutable aspect of the divine purpose. This purpose is perceived in Christianity as the ultimate union of perfected man with the Godhead, and such spiritual perfection is attained only through suffering. The idea of heavenly purpose is necessary because it enables us to rationalize the experiences of life.

Belief in the passibility and empathy of God tends to tolerance of global affliction; belief in the impassibility of God encourages aloofness from suffering. These contradictory ideas lead to the denial of compassion, but apathy that allows suffering without compassion and 'permitted evil' without responsibility, inflicts suffering on God. The divine empathy is a mystery but as God participates in creation and shares our suffering, God also shares the experience of evil that causes affliction. Humankind abrogates responsibility for stewardship when it is claimed that the global affliction, inflicted upon each other, is part of God's purpose. A theodicy of immanence affirms that God is involved empathetically in the world and is historically present to human suffering in the incarnation. In the life of Jesus the empathy of God is actualized and the transformative power of good demonstrated in the reality of human existence. If we accept an empathetic theodicy it becomes apparent that evil and suffering are borne by God because of divine participation in the world, not as part of God's own nature.

With gradual changes in the understanding of God, changes also take place in the ethical demands set over humankind. The area of responsibility in human affairs expands outwards from the notion of the Garden of Eden to communal conscience as set out in the Decalogue, then to responsibility for a new order envisioned by Jesus; concern for the close neighbour extended beyond the Mosaic Law to encompass the 'distant enemy' and, today, extends beyond the parish to the Third World.

Changing concepts about God resulted in a paradoxical understanding of the nature of God as being both transcendent and immanent. Consequently the integration of opposite attributes into our understanding of God, and God's relationship to the world, changes the possible theodicies which attempt to equate the presence of evil with Christian beliefs. While God may be omnipotent, he is free as a self-existent Being, to choose to surrender control over creation. A God who has created a world 'far more precarious and destructive than necessary' it is argued, is a God beyond the categories that human beings could trust, because although he has the power to control and reverse events, 'we cannot be sure that he will choose to do so'.[5] The transcendence of God does not answer the human need for the understanding of global affliction and so we become aware of a gulf in the relationship between God and his creatures. If God retains ultimate control of the universe, as it is believed, then it may be justified to blame God for the presence of evil in human existence. If we relate theodicy to the transcendence of God then we necessarily become aware of living in the nuclear age as a time when God does not demonstrate his concern for the world.

This view is contradicted by those who argue that the biblical God is neither impassible and remote from the world, nor separated from us by an unbridgeable void. According to Yung Lee, God affirms the 'goodness' of creation by sharing human suffering with us – otherwise the creation would not be good. When evil in the world blocks out the participation of God's love, he is made to suffer estrangement which is the divine response to sin. That evil is the cause of estrangement would accord with the idea that God has turned his back on the affliction of humanity since Hiroshima; but a theodicy of immanence tells us that the suffering of the world through intentional evil and by 'permitted evil' is also inflicted upon God. God's suffering is intensified by divine empathy: 'since the intensity of suffering is proportionate to the intimacy of relationship, the God who relates himself unconditionally to love the world is the greatest sufferer of all'.[6] The God who wills to participate in the world to preserve the goodness of creation, suffers *with us*.

4. *The God of providence*

The understanding of history as under the providential direction of God has always been a feature of Judaeo-Christianity. Significant events have been reinterpreted in the past to show the *positive* side of providence. Theodicy in the nuclear age should undertake a similar shift of perception. Theodicists are confronted with the relationship between evil and God's will and the attempt to understand the place of evil in God's world. The inconsistency between a providential God of love and the undeniable evil in human history found one resolution in the doctrine of 'original sin'; but if we reject responsibility for our actions we also abrogate freedom of will. Such a doctrine no longer satisfies theodicists today, who claim that evil was part of the *risk* taken by God in bringing the world into being.

If it is accepted that God does intervene in the world of human experience it is even more puzzling to consider some episodes in contemporary history where God has chosen not to intervene. As Maurice Wiles points out, where death and natural disasters are frequent, believers hold to the impassibility of God, but where such incidents are seen as an inexorable and impersonal law of the universe, God is apprehended as free, personal being. Human understanding of God's relation to the world must be affected by historical and cultural context of its time. In the history of Christian thought God, while being praised for goodness, has been disassociated from evil and responsibility for it; but the atrocities of the twentieth century challenge such a theodicy and the primary question has moved from the activity of God to an understanding of his nature. Advances in historical and scientific knowledge have made faith in divine agency problematic and God's action in relation to secondary causes no longer convincing. Wiles continues: 'If evil is somehow inherent in the creative process, so too must be the overcoming of that evil.'[7]

Although the conviction that God has the power to intervene in the world derives from his involvement in the history of the Israelites and the resurrection, was that action compatible with the changelessness of God? Can such a belief be maintained in the modern world and what kind of divine act would be understandable to sceptical, scientifically oriented human beings? Has such an event already occurred with the advent of nuclear fission? The task of theodicy today is to reinterpret nuclear developments as *more* significant for the future of the world than may be evident at the moment.

It is posited by Yung Lee that the attribute of impassibility in the nature of God is inconsistent with the Christian concept of a compassionate God. Arguing from the Johannine statement, 'God is love' (I John 4.8, 11), Lee shows that *agape* is not merely an attribute or function of God but the very nature of God. Love is what God does to us through participation in human experience. Lee draws his concept of divine empathy from the dialectical tension in the relationship between God and the world. In the activity of *agape* God is both transcendent and immanent and this tension creates a condition of passibility in the inner life of God. The participation of *agape* in the world is much greater than sympathy and is understood theologically as 'the drive toward the reunion of the separated'. The empathy of God is defined by Lee as the participation of divine feeling into human feeling so that unity of feeling is attained.

Process theologians resolve the problem of the transcendence and immanence of God by perceiving the relationship between God and humanity as that of *co-creation*. The relationship of God to the world requires a third dimension, that of human commitment in an active encounter rather than in a subjective and contingent role. If the nature of God could be understood as a dynamic *response* to the world, instead of a series of static attributes, perhaps we could understand that God is within the whole of creation, infusing and informing all the activity of the world with his being. As human consciousness develops to realize more of the universe and its interrelatedness the understanding of God must also change. The insight of process theology requires that instead of objectifying evil in the world, human beings need to make a reappraisal of the inter-relatedness of human activity with the will of God. The dynamic idea of reality as flowing eternal activity accords with the hypothesis of evolution and the discoveries of modern science. It challenges the traditional concepts of a God with changeless attributes and provides a scenario in which God is not only creator and sustainer of the world, but also the positive director of an unfolding reality. This theodicy understands God as creative persuasion, acting as a 'lure' towards the good in human intention but allowing freedom to respond to that direction. It changes the ideas of immanence and transcendence to that of God and humanity co-creating in relation-ship.

A further aspect of the concept of God as a being 'whose versatility of becoming is unlimited, whose potentialities of content embrace all possibilities, whose sensitive responsiveness surpasses that of all other individuals' is that God's actuality is *altered* with every change of the actual state of the world.[8] The philosophy of A. N. Whitehead reinterprets the paradoxical attributes of trans-cendence and immanence in the nature of God as interdependent process, in which existence itself grows out of previous processes. In this understanding of reality God, humanity and existence are part of the same pattern and nothing can be separate. Therefore we are jointly responsible with God for the shaping of our future.

Cosmic Purpose in Evolutionary Perspective

J. MacDonald Smith

1. *If it moves, shoot it*

'The scientists are not masters of the destiny of science; the changes they bring about may, without their knowing it, force them into positions they would never have chosen. Their curiosity and its effects may be stronger than their humainity.' So said the eminent scientist J. D. Bernal in 1929 in a prophetic statement whose meaning was most clearly revealed on the occasion of the explosion of the first atomic bomb. On that day, in a telling phrase, science knew sin: humanity was required to resolve the life or death dilemma implicit from the start in the use of technology.

I know exactly what this means: four years work at the Atomic Weapons Research Establishment, Aldermaston, on some of the effects of atomic and hydrogen bombs has left me with moral and spiritual scars, together with a conviction that this is not what science is for. Every time a newspaper carries yet another item on cancers related to those weapons' trials of the fifties, or on the cynical disregard for the native populations of the areas in which they were held, or on the reasons why the bombs were dropped on Japan, it reinforces this conviction.

Even in those early days when we were busily proliferating nuclear weapons on behalf of the United Kingdom my colleagues and I felt torn: on the one hand we were engaged in some temptingly fascinating research which we could have done nowhere else; on the other hand honestly to face the purpose of our work was to lift the lid on a vision of hell. My father, who ended the Second World War responsible for Radar research for the RAF, had taught me that science was a humanely beneficent activity practised in order to deepen our understanding of the universe and to improve the human lot – a kind of socially responsible curiosity. But he would cynically contrast his work of saving life with mine of destroying it. When, after a lapse of twenty years, I took training as a Civil Defence scientific adviser it was even clearer how right he was, for not even the Home Office in its official training of those who were going to help restore 'normal' life after a nuclear war could disguise the hopelessness of the task.

I said that we measured 'some of the effects' of atomic and hydrogen bombs. That is to say we measured the immediate destructive effects in terms of megatonnage of weapons along with heat, radiation and so on. What we did not measure because we had no real data (though I do remember a department hopefully called 'Health Physics') were the long-term effects. This disregard for the public has been exposed by recent enquiries into weapons-testing related cancers, and also by revelations connected with a headlong and ill-thought-out rush to develop nuclear energy. The fire at Windscale, the Chernobyl disaster, problems with the disposal of nuclear waste, and data on the enhanced levels of leukaemia in the vicinity of nuclear establishments have raised questions about the nature of the genie which has emerged from this particular bottle. Thus, the observed unexpected general increase of cancer which began in the sixties points to a connection with our nuclear activity. As there is no safe level of radiation below which no undesirable effects appear, any increase in radiation levels is bound to result in increased cancers, mutations and the like.[1] Moreover, any increase in nuclear activity results in enhanced radiation levels unless extremely expensive precautions are taken (we could, for instance, safely dispose of nuclear waste by sending it to the sun – a peaceful use of rocket technology). The 'levels of safety' which are proudly referred to by British Nuclear Fuels Limited and the Radiological Protection Board are 'nukespeak' for they are in fact rough guesses at how many people will die as a result of equally rough guesses at the pollutive effects of a given reactor programme. One sees this mixture of technological 'frontiersmanship' and the lust for profit time and again – think of the Bhopal disaster – where a perfectly sound idea is hurriedly embraced without proper precautions, and everybody is wise after the event.

There need be no argument that the nuclear predicament is an irresponsible use of technology in short-term interests. But it is not the only threat: the environmental and ecological crisis is related and it too has to be resolved for it could easily prove to be as serious. Human beings along with many other species could yet go out with an ecological whimper rather than a nuclear bang as pollution gradually poisons the planet, overuse of resources eventually starves it and human overpopulation rapidly increases the effects of both.

Technological Luddism is not an appropriate reaction, for science has and can still benefit mankind as we develop a better understanding of the cosmos. It is possible to distinguish very roughly between two kinds of technology: Rustum Roy designates them Science Based Technology (SBT) and International Technology (IT).[2] The former is the activity of the ten or twenty per cent of the world's scientists who, motivated by a sense of social responsibility or vocation, are seeking to apply the scientific understanding of the principles that underlie the world for the good of all. SBT is humanitarian in outlook and its values are very much the same as those of religion. Much of medical science is SBT; so is appropriate technology, navigational aids and the development of communications systems in general. International Technology, however, is a parasite. Its values are profit, aggression and exploitation: it is science under the control of the multinationals and the financiers. IT can be characterized by the phrase 'science for profit', where SBT would be more aptly described as 'science for people'.

Science's contribution to a multifocal understanding of reality, allied to a recast theology, could in SBT result in what Capra has described as 'a radically different social and economic structure', even if his own attempt to set this out is somewhat theoretical.[3]

SBT has wrongly been seen as a threat to religion. But IT *is* the new religion: faithfulness to this 'god' provides 'security' through 'deterrence'; it ensures that your days will be long in the land as you cower behind 'nuclear defence' and eventually your Star Wars screen. IT arises from the assumption that Spaceship Earth is an infinite resource to be plundered, an infinitely large dustbin for the disposal of waste. Yet like all megalomaniac idols it will not face up to the fact that in nuclear weaponry it has met its match and cannot control an offspring more evil than itself. Typically, it thinks that more of the same in SDI will manage the problems it has given itself. On the other hand, serious investment in SBT could solve many of the world's problems and certainly lessen the threat of war in doing so.

This can be summarized: IT sees nature as an adversary to be overpowered and exploited for profit; SBT sees nature as an ally to be understood for the sake of people.

2. *From hypergrowthmania to peace with justice and freedom*

We turn now to a consideration of the interrelationship of theology and science as a preparation for the final section which offers a model of God for the nuclear age.

If a theological scheme is to have any integrity at all it has no right of appeal to the arbitrary, miraculous or apparently inexplicable. That there are mysteries is undeniable, but unless one is going to come clean about the 'God of the gaps' error the pending tray for these is not marked 'theology'. Einstein once remarked that 'God who creates and is nature is very difficult to understand, but he is not arbitrary or malicious.'

We shall therefore begin with the world and with our normal, pure science way of understanding it. We take a conservative position as our starting point with that assessment of the material order which was such a relief to David Hume and which Anthony Flew calls the Stratonician Presumption.[4] This can be expressed in the words, 'Whatever characteristics we think ourselves able to discern about the universe as a whole are the underivative characteristics of the universe itself'. A roughly equivalent statement would be my own: 'It is the case that things in the universe behave in an intelligibly rational manner in accordance with their natures'.[5]

From the theological point of view this has to be so. The tradition speaks of an omnipotent, rational and free creator, which implies that creation is contingent in nature and intelligibly rational. Since it could be other than it is in every respect then clearly experiment is the only way to find out how it actually is. This is fundamental: there is no possibility of *deducing* the structure of the universe from a collection of *a priori* principles, even if these have experimental justification. This methodological principle should be born in mind when we come to consider the bases of mathematics and of theology.

But what does experiment do? On many occasions it has been observed that when hot and cold bodies are juxtaposed, the hot body gets cooler and the cold one warms up. Does this justify the claim that in the future this will always be so?

Half a century ago this worried the philosopher of science, Karl Popper, as it had two centuries ago worried the philosopher Hume. 'Hume's Problem', the problem of induction, asks the question whether, if a given set of circumstances has always hitherto resulted in the same consequences, are we entitled to claim that it always will do so? Are all swans white?

There is another problem concerning the logical connection, if any, between physical theory and the experimental data upon which theory rests. Briefly, there is none. The relationship is an aesthetic one between experimental data and 'elegant' theory, for it is possible to put an infinite number of curves through a finite set of points on a graph. Experiment therefore does not prove theory; what it does is not disprove it. Yet experiment is the only way there is to get information about the material order. It looks as if we are in trouble.

This raises the issue of the objectivity of science as an activity which actually does describe real features of a real world, or whether it can be described in an equivalent way to that in which M. E. Spiro described religion as 'a cultural system consisting of culturally patterned interactions with culturally postulated super-human beings.'[6] But as Peacocke says, it is unlikely that a reductionist view of science will worry anyone who is not a cosmologist or particle physicist (which a lot of people are) and that most scientists will continue to adopt a critical realist attitude, continuing to believe that the things they talk about do exist even if they are imperfectly understood. (This does not mean, however, that they are necessarily right.) Yet the sociology of knowledge is also relevant for science: Mary Hesse, for instance, makes a very good case for holding that the criterion of success and hence of 'truth' in science is success in prediction and control. Unlike the alchemists of old we have learnt how to make the right moves which ensure increased adaptation to our environment. In the light of the previous section of this essay there is clear reason to doubt our success. On this criterion we are not even very good at science.

Popper draws out the consequences of Hume's Problem. Insights into nature cannot be summed up to order because they occur by a psychological process of which we are largely ignorant. Experiment does not confirm these insights – it simply does not contradict them. In consequence scientific knowledge is *ad hoc*, and its progress is to be compared with pushing piles into a swamp until they are secure enough to bear the weight which it is intended they should bear.[7]

Hence, Popper develops his most important idea, that of *falsifiability*; scientific statements are those which are empirically falsifiable, and all empirically falsifiable statements are scientific statements. Falsifiability is therefore a *criterion of demarcation* and not a criterion of meaning, truth or knowledge. This is fundamental.

Thus we arrive at an interim understanding of the nature of reality by setting up falsifiable hypotheses for which there are already some grounds – the criterion of *corroboration*. Clearly no scientific statement can express absolute truth. On the other hand, no scientific statement ought to be infallibly true, for if so it would be both unfalsifiable and uninformative.

We have indicated that all statements which 'must be true' in the sense that it is impossible for 'x not to be the case', are uninformative. This is a consequence of a branch of mathematics called Information Theory which has been very helpful in the computer field. Informative statements are contingent; they or their consequences will be empirically falsifiable. This does not imply a dismissal of other disciplines as meaningless or untrue for Popper makes clear that non-scientific statements are valid and true knowledge. Among these are mathematics and logic, poetry and painting, and of course, theology. I am going to suggest that in some important respects theological language is more akin to that of mathematics and logic than it is to that of physics and chemistry.

In mathematics and logic a set of symbols is interrelated in accordance with rules. A formal system is then set up on a basis of a small number of axioms (the 'assumptions') from which may be derived the large number of consequences (the 'truths' of the system). The system is not 'about' anything except perhaps itself, and is simply a collection of marks on paper arranged in obedience to rules which are as 'conventional' as the marks. The system as a whole cannot be said to be true; and the concept which is invoked in place of 'truth' is that of 'consistency', in that in a consistent system none of the consequences of the axioms will contradict any of the others.

This may appear abstract. Yet it describes the mathematics which when applied in pure science, makes possible the analysis of the models through which comprehension of the physical world is attained. If a mathematical system is not about anything, it can be applied to nearly everything because it cannot be invalidated by hard fact.

The fundamental theological statement 'God exists' is not empirically falsifiable – and *empirical* falsifiability is the only kind there is. The same can be said of the statement 'God does not exist'. Therefore atheism and the hypothecation of God are alike untrue. This does not, however, apply to *models* of God which are modifiable in the light of circumstances. But the statement 'God exists' is infallibly true and therefore by a result previously noted, uninformative.

So like pure mathematics and logic, pure theology is not a set of informative statements about how things are in reality. In any given theological system it is a set of symbols which are operative in accordance with the rules of the system, which in turn is based on a small number of theological axioms. Any given theological system will consist of meaningful statements which are true knowledge and of potentially universal applicability. But it is not 'about' anything. Like mathematics it is a way through to an understanding of reality: in this case a method of creating models of reality.

A number of interesting consequences for theology in a nuclear world arise from this analysis.

The first consequence relates to the possibility of a shift from religions in the plural to religion in the singular. If theology cannot be taken as a set of informative statements about reality, then all that prevents all the stories told by all religions from being entertained by all believers is a triumphalist attitude on the part of some believers. This is not a plea that a universal world religion be invented, which would be artificial and would limit still further the myths, stories and models with which religion motivates human aspirations. It is, however, to suggest that there are rational grounds for the followers of any religion to take the followers of another religion and their models as seriously as they take fellow-believers in their own religion and that religion's models, and in all respects.

A second consequence for Christian theology is that it will shift its centre of gravity from beliefs *about* Jesus to the beliefs *of* Jesus, making use of models of Jesus which shed light on these. This is not to say that metaphors such as King, Son of God, Son of Man, and models like incarnation will disappear, for models and metaphors are the stuff of religion. But they will not be used in quite the same ways as hitherto, and especially so in the light of the valuing of many different religious ways of understanding. Other religions would need to make corresponding adjustments to their doctrinal schemes.

Finally there is an ethical consequence involved in a theological response to the nuclear predicament. The threat to the planet may well be eroded piecemeal by a spiritual, ethical and moral climate generated by a multiplicity of religious choices which, whatever else is the case, has this in common: that it views IT and all its works as evil and wishes the planet well.

The nuclear age forces us to make a quantum jump in religious understanding.

3. *Darwin developed: and the sound of the wings of the morning*

The central affirmation of theism – belief in God – remains unchanged in a world which faces the threat of International Technology. However, changes are necessary in our understanding of the logical status of talk about God. If traditional models of God have become inappropriate, then change also affords opportunities of developing new ones. In this section an alternative model is offered in terms of embodied cosmic purpose, and its ethical consequences are developed.

Julian Huxley tells us that humanity is at the beginning of a new evolutionary step. So far there have been three main evolutionary leaps, and Huxley names the fourth step as the era of self-consciously purposive evolution. The preceding three phases have been the inorganic, which led to the emergence of 'living' collocations of macromolecules; then came the biological phase culminating in the emergence of *homo sapiens*; and following this there was the phase of psycho-social evolution with the development of human culture. We are now entering a new phase in which the evolutionary process says Huxley, '. . . has for the first time become aware of itself, is studying the laws of its own unfolding, and has a dawning realization of the possibilities of its own future guidance or control. In other words, evolution is on the verge of becoming internalized, conscious and self-directing.'[8] At the least it can be said that purposiveness is embedded in the cosmos (it would perhaps be too much to suggest that the cosmos itself is in some sense a purposeful organism) and in human beings is achieving the possibility of self-determination.

If purposiveness is a valid model of God then here is clear evidence of cosmic divine activity with men and women being invited into co-creatorship. A development of a model for incarnation is useful here, for I am suggesting a creative process whereby the power to create has embodied itself within the material order. As God has been said in Christian theology to have assumed humanity inseparably and eternally in Jesus, so on our model the material order is inseparably assumed in the act of creation. It is inseparable because that act is not a 'one-off' past event from the results of which God who initiated it can be separated (there is no evidence in science or theology for this, essentially deistic position) but an eternal sustaining of the material order leaving both the creator and the material order with their integrity intact in an unconfused and eternal unity.

Another way of seeing this model is on the analogy of the self and the body between which there is also unconfused unity. The self acts through an evolving and developing and everchanging body without which it could not be itself; the body needs the self to give it life and

135

would not without the self have any awareness of itself as existing. On our model God is incarnated in the material order as the self is in the body and works through the material order as the self works through the body. The Divine self-awareness will then be mediated through the material order of the cosmos and its purposes expressed in and through the cosmos.

Let us explore in more detail the nature of cosmic purpose. There is a theory in physics which states that systems tend to disintegrate, and anybody with a house to maintain knows exactly what that means. Why then since the universe is so old, does it appear that at least in one small corner of it events have gone in exactly the opposite direction? Why even if this did take an astronomically long time, did Coventry Cathedral, the Beatles, Einstein or whatever emerge when physics is quite clear that the probability of any one of these occurrences is so small that it ought never to have happened at all?

Perhaps the most serious challenge to this notion of immanent purpose has been offered by Jacques Monod.[9] His argument boils down to the idea that the right atoms met each other purely by chance in the primordial soup to produce an entity with the power to reproduce itself. Such dogmatism cannot be sustained, however, for Monod himself writes of 'a sickness of the spirit, the most serious outcome of the ideational evolution which created and increasingly worsens it' – a value judgment which does not lend support to his thesis.

From another perspective Wigner shows that the mathematical probability of the spontaneous formation of a self-replicating system out of an assemblage of component parts is zero.[10] Plainly, he and Monod cannot both be right. If Wigner is right then very small probabilities point to immanent purpose rather than to an accidental arrival of all the right components in one place at the same time. Furthermore A. R. Peacocke cites the work of Eigen to show how subtle the interplay of law and chance in the evolution of living species can be, so that the emergence of living creatures is inevitable, ensuring also that they evolve in a creative manner which allows new forms to evolve.[11] It appears in principle impossible either to predict the future course of evolution or to trace back its historical route beyond certain time limits. Immanent purpose is very reasonably attributed to the course of events which we call evolution.

My suggestion is that the cosmos is the 'body' of which God is the purposeful 'self' and that the purpose of creativity is to bring its self-manifestation to a state of such self-awareness as to be able to enter into a partnership of co-creation. Since the Divine self-embodiment encompasses the entire universe (whatever that may turn out to consist of), and since even in that part of the cosmos which is at present in principle detectable from earth there may well be many planets capable of supporting life, then the consequences of a human refusal to measure up to the demands of the self-consciously purposive phase of its evolution may well be obliteration through nuclear war and the fulfilment of creative purpose elsewhere in the universe. There are no grounds for human beings to assume that they are a unique species in the universe or that there are not other species through whom the divine purpose can be fulfilled. The random pattern of the evolutionary process is certainly consistent with this thought and the idea of self-consciously purposive evolution does not exclude the possibility of species-destruction – on the contrary it logically includes it.

The race is on against time – can we take the evolutionary step forward before we blow ourselves into extinction? We can return to our starting point. If my father was right to teach me that science is for people not profit, for men and women and not markets, then IT is a dangerous threat to the future of humanity. Our real hope lies in a responsible use of the facts which science discovers in accordance with the values which religion expresses – in other words, with SBT.

This involves an effort on the part of both scientific and religious communities. Both need to learn humility. The scientific community must learn a sense of social responsibility for the uses to which scientific work is put: one is reminded of Nobel's invention of the most lethal explosive of his time and of his guilt over the consequences; but today's stakes are far higher. Our hopes for science should also remain realistic. The Institute for Social Inventions is currently circulating a kind of Hippocratic Oath for scientists, sponsored by leaders in the scientific community, for signature by scientists who will in consequence bind themselves to carry out only life-enhancing work.

If scientists must learn to apply values as well as facts in obedience to a purpose beyond our own, then theologians must learn how to offer an interpretation of such purpose which scientists can understand and by which they will be inspired. Religion is the source of such values as the human race expresses and on it lies the onus of persuading people to express more of them. Perhaps the best recommendation that can be offered is that theologians and religious believers in general stop talking incomprehensible gobbledegook in small coteries all over the world and start talking to people in language they can understand, about the values which their myths express. After all, values are meant to be turned into hardware.

Humankind is only at the threshold of self-consciously purposive evolution and whether we will cross it remains to be seen. In other language, all are cells in a Divine self-embodiment, called to co-creatorship with a purpose greater than ourselves. It may be that the Peace Movements, the Green Movement and the many pressures for human unity are the beginning of a response to this invitation. We will only survive if we decide to do so as a consequence of deliberately making real changes in our social, political and economic life, and in our religious and moral attitudes. Scientists and theologians alike bear a heavy responsibility to assist an endangered species. The nuclear predicament symbolizes the ultimate bankruptcy of a civilization which thinks of God, humanity and nature as essentially separable.

12

Christian Involvement in an Interfaith Theology of Peacemaking

Alan Race

At the heart of Christian faith there is what can be termed the summons towards a sacred vision of peaceful living, identified in the metaphor of the 'kingdom of God'. This vision is one of human mutuality and interdependence under God, where power serves the needs of people, antagonisms are overcome and justice has become a way of life.

Put like that, the sacred vision is inherently utopian in that it looks for major changes in the corporate body politic and in individual life-styles, in order to turn it into reality. As these changes often seem permanently out of reach, the vision itself remains vulnerable to charges of being impracticable, a 'nice idea' which 'realism' must temper because the world is a nasty place. Yet for Christians the sacred vision is not just a 'nice idea'. Stemming historically from the impact of Jesus, and glimpsed in the present by the religious imagination, the vision has the force of a summons. Dismissing the visionary aspect of 'the kingdom' would have the effect of ignoring this summons.

In the name of 'realism', Christianity has supported many destructive activities, including violence and waging war. But Christianity is not the only religion which has failed to implement its sacred vision of peaceful living. In differing degrees all the major world religions have lent their support to war, and this has generally been justified under variations of the conditions known in Western history as the 'Just War'. But these conditions have never fully been adhered to, and apart perhaps from its application in some wars of liberation, in the nuclear age the notion of the Just War has become redundant.[1]

If the history of the religious support for war is a long and shameful tale, then its legacy is bitter. For the danger is that it continues in the nuclear age in the overall failure of religious communities, their leaders and theologians, to condemn unequivocally the blasphemy of nuclear war and its preparations. Therefore the development of the means for total annihilation by nuclear technology represents a new moment of decision, which not only makes the practical recovery of the sacred vision of peaceful living itself a necessary imperative, but also raises profound theological questions about survival, the meaning of history, and human responsibility for the future.

If the world religious communities are to redeem themselves and contribute towards a new global future, they will need to recover the centrality of the sacred vision of peaceful living that informs the heart of their various messages.

My contention in this essay is that this recovery of sacred vision is best pursued not in isolation, but by a process of *practical collaboration and theological dialogue* between the religions. By collaboration I mean the active practical commitment of people of different religions working together for the sake of peacemaking, seeking ways of overcoming the forces in our world which threaten destruction, and discovering a shared strength to avert the build-up of weapons of mass destruction. By dialogue I mean the pursuit of theological exchange, mutual witness and shared criticism that combines celebrating the truth from one's own tradition with an openness to different perspectives on religious truth coming from other traditions. Both of these moves receive their urgency from the threat and the promise at the heart of the new nuclear context.

In what follows I shall mainly speak out of the Christian tradition. I shall outline first why I believe a process of collaboration and dialogue to be vital for overcoming religious exclusivism as at least one of the roots of war; second, I shall suggest a model for collaboration and dialogue as a means for carrying the process forward; and finally I shall give some examples of how the theological encounter between Christianity and three different faith

140

communities can now be shaped by the context of the nuclear threat.

1. *Overcoming religious exclusivism*

Most religions have an exclusivist dimension as part of their identity. That is to say, theologically, they see themselves as either the one and only locus of religious truth or the most superior of a number of possibilities. From there it is a short step towards viewing the other as requiring to be confronted and then conquered (be it in a 'Holy War' or a 'Just War'). Thus one of the roots of the religious sanctioning of war lies in the negative theological judgment of religions outside of one's own. (There are also other roots, such as religious ties with nationalism and the state, but these are not our concern here, and are covered in various ways by other essays in this collection.) This is plain to see in biblical history, and it has continued through the centuries in Christian history. Though there is no logical link between religious exclusivism and the support for war, there does seem to have been an inevitability of coincidence between the two throughout history. Religious exclusivism will need to be tackled theologically if this seeming inevitability is to be overcome.

Exclusivism in Christian tradition has a number of strands at its root, perhaps the two most dominant being a view of the concept of 'revelation' which interprets it as a special communication from God, and the doctrine of the incarnation of God in Jesus, indicating a unique presence of the divine life on earth. However, at least three factors have enabled a shift towards a more positive appreciation of other religions in the present generation.

First, the actual experience of encounter with people of different world religions, together with an increased knowledge of their traditions, reveals aspirations and fruits every bit as noble or humane as those in Christianity. The 'households of faith' store immense riches and wisdom which have nurtured civilizations of enduring significance, and will continue to do so, at least so far as we can tell.

Second, at the level of belief, many are beginning to realize how religious beliefs are not simply the product of divine revelation *simpliciter*, but are the result of human endeavours to co-ordinate experience and provide a map of meaning for the human spirit. Modern historical consciousness has made us aware of the mundane nature of our religious symbols, their link with historical reality and the indirect measure of their truth. Revelation, in the sense defined above, now looks untenable as a back-up for claims of religious superiority.

Third, critical biblical studies have made us aware of the hermeneutical complexity involved in applying biblical solutions to present-day problems. Texts, we now realize, are not free-floating truths, but arise out of and reflect the concerns of the time and period in which they were written. In this light the Christian appropriation of Jesus as the 'final' revelation of God in the world has its initial reference against the first-century Jewish eschatological-apocalyptic view of history which looked for a deliverer at the end of time. Two thousand years later, in an environment which has learned historical consciousness and strives to value multi-cultural complexity, the 'finality' ('uniqueness') of Jesus requires quite drastic revision.

Taken together, these three factors present a powerful case for a change in the Christian approach to people of other religions. There is no basis now for the theology which fostered the rejection of demonization of the other, such that it could easily lead to sanctioning war. Presumably other religious communities could take similar steps to overcome the sense of exclusivism which has formed part of their identity.

2. *A model for collaboration and dialogue*

The simplest way to eliminate religious exclusivism would be to posit a basic pluralist hypothesis. This would recognize the validity of the different world religious perspectives within which human beings are working out their sacred vision of peaceful living. Each is built upon genuine religious experience, and each has generated different philosophical, theological and ethical traditions as part of their life. The differences between them are due in part to the different experiences and conceptualizations that flow from, and in some degree, depend on the basic experience. God, or perhaps we should say 'Ultimate Reality' (in order to encompass the non-theistic traditions), is both known and unknown in all traditions, and this lends support to the basic pluralist hypothesis itself.

'Ultimate Reality' is both the hidden divine reality animating varied global human religious life, and also the known religious reality imaged under many forms. Faith is not the property of any one religious group alone. The pluralist hypothesis recognizes the wider validity of world religious diversity as a key partner in theological reflection and action. Christian norms are one set of norms among others.[2]

Some might feel unhappy with this proposal because it seems to conjure up some common universal reference point underneath or outside the very different forms of religious beliefs and practices in the world. It may be in danger of so relativizing religious truth that there are no criteria for judging between the religions. Therefore, in order to off-set these very real dangers, there is a need to inject into the model a sense of *critical complementarity* between the traditions. This entails that each tradition has its own experiential and historical uniqueness so that none is reducible to the other, yet each can be accepted as in some way complementary to the other and live in dialectical tension with it.

In order that the pluralist model might be sharpened up, I suggest that the threat of annihilation by nuclear technology should be seen as the major focus around which the *critical complementarity* is pursued. As models require continual testing, part of the testing here could be how well it functions both to foster dialogue in the search for theological truth and to encourage collaboration in the search for practical ways of peacemaking in response to the nuclear threat.

There is some similarity between this proposal and that of the Roman Catholic theologian Paul Knitter in his essay, 'Toward a Liberation Theology of Religions' in *The Myth of Christian Uniqueness*. Nervous about conjuring up a 'common essence' within or behind the religions, Knitter substitutes a soteriological basis for collaboration and dialogue in the liberation 'option for the poor':

Still, by applying the criteria of liberative praxis, by asking, for example, how a particular Hindu belief or Christian ritual or Buddhist practice promotes human welfare and leads to the removal of poverty and to the promotion of liberation, we might be able to arrive at communal judgments concerning what is true or false, or what is preferable, among different religious claims or practices.[3]

In this suggestion Knitter claims to have a 'heuristic device' for a new meeting between religions: 'an approach, a context, a starting point that must itself be clarified as it clarifies and creates new common ground of understanding.'

My own proposal differs in two respects from Knitter's. First, the major soteriological criteria for estimating the relationship between religions I wish to centre around is their response to the crisis of our threatened extinction by nuclear catastrophe. In the nuclear age, liberation from the totality of threatened extinction has every reason to claim our utmost attention, as liberation from the threat which holds the whole planet to ransom. While this is not the main source of immediate threat for many peoples throughout the world, it nevertheless can claim a priority for those (mainly Western powers) who bear responsibility in these matters. Second, it is less nervous about the hypothesis that the one divine reality does animate the different world traditions. Of course we cannot know if this is the case, but neither is the hypothesis *qua hypothesis* impossible. The pluralist model can be tested, and the major criteria for testing will be soteriological, as in Knitter's proposal.

I am suggesting that peacemaking has both practical and theological components: collaboration and dialogue belong together. This is so because dialogue itself harbours some expectation about the relationship between religions at the level of theological truth; and without collaboration in the practical task of peacemaking, religious truth runs the risk of remaining overly idealistic. Yet collaborators and dialogists seldom stay long in the space between them. For a durable theology of peacemaking to emerge this lack will need to be transcended.

3. *Three dialogues in a nuclear context*

An inter-faith theology of peacemaking might begin by calling out, comparing and sharing the non-violent summons at the heart of the religious visions of peaceful living. But identifying the 'sacred vision of peaceful living' is far from being sufficient in the nuclear context. For the nuclear age brings its own special challenges, affecting our theological and ethical beliefs. This is not to say that the non-violent traditions of the religions will not be a rich depository for theological use in the present; so much cannot be gainsaid. Yet wih the 'totality' of the threat posed by the possibility of nuclear war, religious symbols have been placed under the most radical scrutiny. Their power for sustaining life, for enabling us to live with and discover the possibility of renewal in the darkness, and for confronting the powers of personal and political pessimism, must be investigated afresh.

How might this apply in terms of a Christian involvement in an inter-faith theology of peace? By way of illustration I would like to single out three inter-connected features of the new context around which dialogue might take place: first, the relationship of ultimate reality to human responsibility; second, the power of religious symbols to sustain human beings in 'thinking the unthinkable'; third, the possibility of religious symbols as a vehicle for human empowerment and practical involvement. These three features I shall illustrate by way of Christian dialogue with aspects of Buddhism, Judaism, and Hinduism respectively.

'Our modest role,' says Jonathan Schell, 'is not to create but only to preserve ourselves.'[4] Even in this minimal light, the theological issue turns on the degree to which a religion is affirmative of history and the future. That is to say, religions which deny human beings their capacity for responsibility in determining their destiny are unlikely to 'ring true' in the nuclear age. The *Christian-Buddhist dialogue* might bring this aspect of theological responsibility into sharp focus here. This is especially so as Christian incarnational theism has often been hailed as affirming the value of history most clearly, in that history is accepted as the arena of God's creating and saving activity (though it inherited much of this from its parent religion, Judaism); while Buddhism, with its beliefs in No-thing-ness and Emptiness, has been interpreted to be the most history-denying of all the religions. The contrast of course is a false one, as can be seen from historical observation: Christianity has often fostered escapist forms of religion, and Buddhism is first and foremost a religion of ethical praxis, and the religion which has the best record in lending the least support for war. Might it be that these two great religions display contrasting yet complementary insights around the theme of the affirmation of the historical world, and especially its future?

There will be things for both sides to learn. On the one hand, Christians must learn to see the Buddhist outlook as history-affirming. By diagnosing 'thirsting greed' (tanha) as the cause of the central problem of human existence, suffering (dukkha), the Buddha gave human beings total responsibility over their individual and collective destiny. But linked with 'thirsting greed' is ignorance of our true human condition, which is that we are creatures of 'no-self' (anatta), non-independent of others, and impermanent. Realizing the connection between ignorance, greed and suffering will lead to release and Nirvana, and inspire self-renunciation as the basis for moral action. If human assertiveness lies behind the motivation towards war, perhaps it is no accident that Buddhism has succeeded more than most religions in refusing to lend its support for war.

On the other hand, Christianity will have its own experience to offer Buddhists. If Buddhism is the most thorough-going form of the *via negativa* then the Christian experience of life as gift can inspire a sense in which the mundane world counts for something real in spite of its impermanence, where the I-Thou relationship has validity, and where the world is a place of real if not wholly predictable process. Not only suffering but evil also is real, and is to be confronted in spite of the risks of encouraging personal and group ego. In this regard the Christian picture of the crucified Jesus contains its own power of self-renunciation as the means of confrontation with evil and the basis for moral action.

Reflecting on the relation between Christianity and Buddhism in the nuclear context, the Japanese Christian theologian, Kosuke Koyama, writes: 'Theology must engage itself in a task of relating the Buddha's teaching on battle against human greed and the agitated mind of the God of Israel. . . .' As this happens we can note that the two responses to the world – Christian delight and Buddhist negation – both have their own strengths and weaknesses. In dialogue they can be brought into proper dialectical partnership, mutually corrective, recognizing, as Koyama says, 'two different yet intertwined understandings of the history of human greed'.[5]

146

My second example of inter-faith dialogue is the *Christian-Jewish encounter*, especially in the light of the experience of the Jewish Holocaust of the Second World War. The theological confusions, heart-searchings, and trauma in the Jewish soul since the Holocaust belong also with the Christians, for at least two reasons. The first, by direct implication, is on account of the historical Christian complicity in anti-Judaism; and the second, by indirect anticipation, is that the destruction in the Holocaust of the Jews, can be seen as an analogue of global destruction in the Nuclear Holocaust of Humankind. This second dialogue, therefore, asks us to stare into the abyss of annihilation itself.

One of the most searching critiques of Christianity, in the light of its history of anti-Semitism, has been given by Rosemary Radford Ruether. She points out why Christian anti-Judaism is not a peripheral issue:

> Theologically anti-Judaism developed as the left hand of Christology. That is to say, anti-Judaism was the negative side of the Christian affirmation that Jesus was the Christ.[6]

In other words, the Christian rejection of the Jews (a rejection later established in civil law) stems from the penetrating Jewish critique of Christianity that the public signs of the kingdom which would accompany the coming of the Messiah were not publicly available with and after Jesus. Christianity had subsequently to meet the objection with persecution. If Ruether is correct here, then the most thorough-going reconstruction of christology is required. It will need to account for the newness of Jesus in a way which does not demonize the Jews, and which recognizes the total Jewishness of Jesus himself. It will need to extricate the triumphalism so often associated with the doctrine of the incarnation. As triumphalism has led to Holocaust once, there is no reason to think that it will not be repeated. There is a very real danger in one powerful manifestation of Christian faith in the present, associated with the American political and religious New Right, which continues to link the christological triumphalism of Jesus in his second coming with the Holocaust of a nuclear war.[7]

The second feature in Christian-Jewish dialogue picks up the analogical connection between two kinds of Holocaust. The Jewish experience has alerted us to the horizon of utter abandonment and negativity. The Holocaust is an event which the Jewish writer, Arthur Cohen, has called the 'Tremendum', a 'monument out of time', counting as 'metaphysical evidence that discloses something new about our relation to God and God's relation to creation.'[8] Although Cohen would object to us viewing the Jewish Holocaust as an analogue of the potential nuclear version, I believe it is legitimate to do so, for existential and theological reasons. In terms of sheer human impact, the stunned Jewish mind is the stunned mind of all of us. In terms of the theological implications, as Cohen says: 'The *tremendum* has smashed the presumptive self-declaration of secure (Jewish) orthopraxy; it has no less smashed Christian orthodoxy.'[9] The nuclear age, some Christian scholars have said, presents us with a similar dilemma: bluntly, how to believe in the face of abandonment and negativity? Only a suffering God will do, said Bonhoeffer from his Nazi prison. So says many a Jewish reflection on God since the Holocaust. Even then, it can feel like clutching at straws. There may be a point of dialogue between Christians and Jews around the Jewish sense of abandonment by God in the Holocaust, and the Christian sense of the negativity of crucifixion as a focus for what God is up to in our world. It will not be an easy dialogue because of the way in which the cross has functioned in Christian history as a symbol of Jewish rejection. But once abandon that gross misreading and a profound complementarity about how God might be interpreted through death could ensue.

My third example of dialogue centres around the figure of Mahatma Gandhi, and therefore embraces *Christian-Hindu inter-action*. This restores a practical edge to the purpose of an inter-faith theology of peacemaking, for Gandhi was above all someone for whom religious peacemaking was a wholistic way of living, which involved commitment to political change. At the risk of overstating the case it would not be unfair to describe Gandhi as embodying several kinds of dialogue: between theory and practice in religion, between respect for inherited tradition and being radically imaginative in constructing a view of the religious life which answers the needs of the present, and between Christianity and Hinduism.

Anticipating the nuclear holocaust forces us to think of the religious sanction for action in the present in order to avert it. ('Daddy, what are you doing to stop the next war?') If Gandhi's wholistic vision was a complex web of many strands, then chief among these strands was his self-contructed principle of *satyagraha* – 'truth-force', or 'struggle for truth'. It combined elements of the traditional Jain, Buddhist and Hindu stress on non-violence (*ahimsa*), civil disobedience and resistance, the Christian Sermon on the Mount, the disinterested service recommended by the *Bhagavad Gita*, commitment to the search for the unifying spiritual principles of all life, and the recognition that all our views are but fragments of the greater Truth which eludes us all. Above all, it was the pragmatic aspects of the vision which Gandhi held in the foreground:

> (Gandhi) quickened the conscience of men of goodwill professing a variety of traditions and faiths, reminding them of the path of self-sacrifice and love [10]

Gandhi, therefore, was a true liberationist. But in the nuclear age, his non-violent technique meets its severest test. Is it possible that non-violent resistance can be used effectively to bring about both a renunciation of dependence on nuclear weapons as a means of 'defence', and also a form of civil non-co-operation should an enemy invade a country? To many the very idea will seem utterly unrealistic. Nevertheless, the memory of Gandhi retains a glimmer of that possibility. In the face of potential total destruction, could it be that non-violence can at last become the cardinal principle in the recovery of the sacred vision of peace?[11]

In the search for a theology of peace*making* Gandhi's stress on the practical effect of religious symbolism as part of its test of truth – hence incorporating what I have called collaboration in peacemaking between the religions – becomes intrinsic to the religious vision itself.

But Gandhi's vision was informed also by theological sources, and it is not unreasonable to see these as a critical complementarity between what he borrowed from Christianity and what he used from his native Jain and Hindu traditions. Out of his Hindu background Gandhi rejected those strands of Christian thought which were narrowly exclusive and spoke of the salvation of the whole world as focussed in one man and one event. It is also a fair observation that *satyagraha* owed as much to Gandhi's contact with the Christian faith, and in particular with the New Testament principle of *agape*, as with the Jain belief in *ahimsa*. But because of his free borrowing from different sources and his own idiosyncratic 'hermeneutic', critical complementarity has a unique flavour with Gandhi. Nonetheless, he does impart a gift to us: 'a technique which blends in an unusually effective way moral and spiritual insights from East and West.'[12]

I have given three examples of Christian involvement in dialogue in order to illustrate what is involved in the forging of an inter-faith theology of peacemaking. Other examples could have been chosen. For example, the dialogue with Islam around the concepts of 'fundamentalism' and 'holy war' (jihad) has enormous implications in the light of the recent history of the Middle East and the rising confidence of Islam throughout the world. On a slightly different tack, the dialogue with Marxism could explore the common human responsibility for the future in the light of shared values. This is being pursued in a number of forms by liberation theologians in Third World countries. It is a dialogue with slightly different contours from the dialogues presented in this essay, different that is in terms of the overall model, because of the rejection of the notion of 'divine' transcendence in Marxism. But at the present time, when the philosophical problems of pluriform values remain extremely puzzling and vexing, there is room for many models and experiments in dialogue.

Given the nuclear predicament, there is no doubting the enormity of the agenda for the future. If the nuclear age represents a sea-change in thinking and acting religiously, then this is exactly what we should expect. If the planet stands under the threat of annihilation because of human blindness, greed, stupidity and sin, then this puts a question mark against all human institutions to date – including the theological institutions – and demands of them a shared commitment to transcend the route which has led us into the nuclear cul-de-sac. The religions have a unique contribution to make to the world to help us find a way out of the dilemma; at least their sacred visions of peaceful living would lead us so to believe.

This unique contribution embraces collaboration and dialogue, and the one implies and demands the other. Without collaboration we ignore the dominant reality of our time – the interconnectedness of all life, and the practical human responsibility to draw back from threat of nuclear annihilation. Without dialogue we ignore the theoretical roots of the suspicion of the other: we risk substituting our relative and partial grasp of religious truth for the Absolute to which it points, thus laying the potential for war in the ideological foundations of superiority as one of its roots. In the space between collaboration and dialogue between religions it is just possible that a theology of peacemaking might be forged.

Such a theology would be hopeful, thoughtful, and practical. It would be hopeful because it would begin the process of reversing the history of the religious support for war by abolishing one of war's root causes. It would be thoughtful because only by stretching the human mind towards fundamental concepts can we begin to appreciate the profound intellectual challenge of the nuclear age. It would be practical because the religious hold on life is at the end of the day practical: if it does not foster the concrete possibility of ethical fruits then the sacred vision of peace remains an illusion and a lie. As it is, we know that the religions have seldom risen to meet their own recommendations.

The dissonance between the religious sacred visions of peaceful living and the wretched sanctification of war through the ages has been so great that many could be forgiven for becoming disillusioned with the religious response to life. From the 'vantage-point' of the totality of destruction, symbolized by nuclear war and its preparations in nuclear weapons development, the religions are forced to face their complicity in war through the ages. Paradoxically, they may at the last be able to turn the potential horror of that 'vantage-point' in the direction of hope, and pursue the sacred vision of peaceful living afresh. If they do, both collaboration and dialogue will be their essential means. There may yet be time.

Christian Witness in the Nuclear State

13

The Idols of Security

Roger Ruston OP

1. *Religious parallels in nuclear deterrence*

The parallel between nuclear deterrence and a particular type of religion has often been pointed out. In the early days (1958) two American authors described it thus:

> The response to this greatest of all triumphs of scientific method and creative intelligence has been in some respects closely akin to the practice of magic among the most primitive of tribes. Having in their possession a fearful image of the god of war, which makes them stronger than all their enemies, the tribe is obsessed with the fear that the image may be stolen or duplicated and their exclusive claim to the deity's favour lost. So a temple is built, ringed about by walls and guarded by untiring sentinels. Those whose function it is to attend the deity are carefully chosen and subjected to purification rites; they are forbidden ever to look upon the whole image or to speak of what they have seen. They are guarded with unceasing vigilance and at the slightest sign of defection condign punishment is visited upon them.[1]

Thirty years on, the parallel is even more striking. Nuclear deterrence resembles the cult of some warrior state now grown into a devouring obsession which eats up more and more human and material resources and threatens to undermine the stability of the state itself – like the cult of Quetzalcoatl in pre-conquestMexico. It has an arcane 'theology' elaborated by a clerical elite (MAD, Flexible Response). It postulates a satanic enemy which can be kept

155

at bay only by resolute practice of the cult. Its guardians claim that, if the image is not perpetually refurbished ('modernized'), there will be a cosmic catastrophe and a return to chaos. The sanitary cordon of purity around the mysteries extends to the minor employees of electronics firms that take on defence contracts. The secrecy in which the principle decisions have been made by tiny groups of politicians entirely outside parliamentary control is legendary. The whole enterprise engenders evasion and lies as standard procedure. Like all centralized tribal or state religions it is fundamentally anti-democratic.

Up to this point the connection between nuclear deterrence and religion may seem metaphorical rather than real – nothing more than a sociological fancy. However, when we move to the moral plane, the connection is seen to be real enough. Consider the moral burden that nuclear deterrence lays on the shoulders of those who make it ready for battle – a burden that is shared by all of us who willingly live under its protection, even if we do not acknowledge our part in it. The practice of nuclear deterrence implies that there is no limit to the amount of destruction we should be prepared to commit in the state's service. It implies that we are ready, on orders from political or military superiors, to destroy totally cities full of civilians, and to make future reconciliation, or even life itself, impossible. It implies also a willingness to destroy God's earthly creation. We will do these things rather than step down in a military confrontation. In doing so we would transgress all known moral limits. But in so far as we are prepared to transgress *all* moral limits in the service of any person or collectivity, we treat them as a god. In a real sense, usually obscured from us by the modern separation of religion and politics, we have fallen into idolatry. We have made a god of the state.

2. *Moral method and idolatry*

Those who are in this position are not short of sincerely-held justifications. They are keeping the peace. They are preventing war. They are resisting the spread of godless communism. The justifications are based upon the assumption that it is not *what* people do, but the *end result* of what they do, that is of final importance. This end result is usually expressed as a balance of evils. There are no actions absolutely wrong in themselves.[2] Yet it is well enough known by everyone that if a fraction of existing nuclear arsenals were to be used, the result could be the deaths of millions of innocent people. However, the argument is that if there were imminent danger of the Soviet forces prevailing in a military conflict in Europe, rather than backing down it would be justified for NATO to use nuclear weapons up to the level of direct attacks on Soviet cities.[3] It would be considered the lesser evil. There are those who would not normally argue this way who nevertheless think that there is no other moral choice open to them when faced with ultimate evils of the kind that is habitually attributed to the Soviet Union.

Several Roman Catholic Bishops' conferences have used arguments from consequences to justify their qualified acceptance of nuclear deterrence – though they have sought to justify *possession* of nuclear weapons rather than their *use*, imagining that the two can be separated for moral purposes.[4] It is a method they would vigorously repudiate in other areas of morality, e.g. sexual ethics and abortion. But church leaders have always tended to revert to utilitarian arguments when dealing with governments. They perhaps consider that they would lose all moral influence over government if they did not – whereas the only way of maintaining influence over the individual faithful is to insist on excluding utilitarian reasoning in personal morality. In adopting such arguments, however, they are falling in with a method that is endemic to political life and which has, since the Second World War, tended to exclude all other kinds of moral reasoning. There are good reasons why consequences have always played a greater part in political morality than in personal morality. Nevertheless, Christian tradition holds that there are limits to such calculations, as codified, for instance, in the rules of just war. These limits provide a vital framework for the professional ethics of state servants when dealing with citizens of their own or foreign states. The prohibition against bombing non-combatants is traditionally one of the most important of these limits. However, there has been a thorough erosion of this moral framework in recent decades. The civilian bombing of World War II, the bombing of Cambodia during the Vietnam war – these and other episodes have been benchmarks in the West's abandonment of its traditional morality. The rise of the National Security State since World War II has provided the political environment in which State security – as interpreted by the government in power – has become the overriding justification for acts that are contrary to national and international law.

3. *The impotence of modern natural law ethics*

Church leaders are not helped in the task of finding an authentically Christian solution by a consensus among liberal Christian ethicists – the so-called 'natural law' moralists – who hold that there can be no distinctive Christian content to political morality. A good example of this occurs in an essay by Professor Gordon Dunstan on 'Theological Method in the Deterrence Debate'.[5] Dunstan's argument is that Christian theologians and public servants who assist in writing reports on matters of public policy should reject the criticism often levelled at them that their reports are 'not Christian enough'. The reason for this is that,

> If the language and meaning of Christianity are to be taken seriously, there are some human activities which cannot be discussed in Christian terms at all.

Among these is the supreme human concern of *security*. Centuries of work on the traditions of natural law and the 'just war' are said to point this way. In all of this work, 'Christians had been operating an essentially human, that is secular discipline . . .' Whereas Israel in the Old Testament had specific national security concerns, the teaching of Jesus, being 'universalistic' in character, deliberately prescinded from all matters of politics. This leaves Christians in a situation where only secular wisdom is available to them in this area: meaning, in effect, a willing co-operation with governments and kings. The upshot is that:

> The work of Christian theologians and moralists today who, in pursuit of security, sit with professional diplomatists, military men and political commentators and explore the problems within their given terms – as they will sit in citizen debate anywhere on

common civic concerns – is entirely consistent with this constitutional tradition. They recognize that theological and exegetical expertise . . . are no substitute for professional competence; and that Christian commitment by no means eases the burden of responsible decision – in the advice given to Ministers of the Crown, for instance, in relation to military or foreign policy – but rather increases it.

What then, is the role of theology in all this? The answer is nothing much, except to remind us that we have certain doctrines about God's relationship with 'man' – especially original sin, and that political activity is as much within the gracious activity of God as any other activity of 'man'. These doctrines dictate on the one side that we must strive for peace, and that on the other we must 'provide for the possibility that peace may fail, in short to arm'. (Not many rulers in history would have disagreed with that.) 'In this good yet disordered human realm there is no security without authority, no authority not ultimately backed by power.' What happens to the theological argument? Instead of adopting the universalist, non-political teaching attributed to Christ as his guide, Dunstan reaches for the supposed particularist, national security concerns of ancient Israel, in order to provide an argument for nuclear deterrence. Christians, he says, are subject to the same paradox as Israel: although God's righteousness will triumph in the end, in this world, evil triumphs all too often. It is necessary to work against it without becoming unrighteous oneself. Nuclear deterrence appears to be founded on the threat to commit unrighteous acts, namely to destroy cities indiscriminately. However, this does not make deterrence itself immoral, since the intention of threatening to use the deterrent is *not* to use it, but to restrain the enemy from a first, provocative use. The moral onus is therefore upon the enemy: 'If, knowing the consequences, he commits that act, the responsibility for the consequences is primarily his, however much the respondent also is to blame: he brings undiscriminating destruction upon his own head, and on all his people.' (This conforms exactly with the British Government's own justification of deterrence.) But this conclusion is neither Christian nor non-Christian. There is, for Professor Dunstan, 'only a choice among evils'.

159

To be fair, many of the things Professor Dunstan says on the way to this arid conclusion are true and salutary reminders of what Christians should not do. They should indeed beware of making short cuts based on faith or biblical texts about love when the situation demands real knowledge of politics and strategy, real rational insight and practical understanding of consequences. However, there are serious draw-backs to this approach. Because the moral method which has been adopted is essentially that dictated by the special ends of politics and strategy, the 'natural law' moralist finds his choices dictated by them too. The 'choice of evils' that he ended up with is inevitably the choice that is proposed by the experts whom he was happy to sit with – in this case the managers of the National Security State. The idea that theology might determine a different choice does not occur.

The consequentialist method, which is perfectly legitimate within the boundaries set by our basic values and traditional wisdom about what should never be done under any circumstances, when extended to the entire field of ethics can only lead to endless accommodation with the powers. One of the noticeable results in the area under discussion is that moral judgments about weapons and strategies get indefinitely postponed in favour of the political decisions of the security managers, who, like the priests of some mystery religion, are the only ones in possession of all the facts which are necessary in order to make 'realistic' judgments. (From time to time, when in debate with officials from the Ministry of Defence, one is told that, if one knew certain classified information which they alone know, one would come to a different conclusion about the necessity of nuclear weapons.) In fact, when the consequentialist method is taken all the way – as it is by some more recent 'natural law' moralists – it means that there can be no specifically *moral* insight, let alone Christian insight, into practical and political problems. Pragmatic choices between evils become the typical predicament in which we are placed, and there is no way of making the relevant distinction between what *happens* and what we *do*, because all decisions are to be made on the basis of some future events regardless of who is responsible for them.

As a result moral choices are left in the hands of the experts, who unfortunately do not have the knowledge of consequences that is attributed to them. As Alasdair MacIntyre has argued, the kind of knowledge which the managerial expert claims and the moralist aspires to simply does not exist.[6] It does not exist because there are major sources of unpredictability in human affairs which are ineradicable. In the case of nuclear deterrence, this consideration is rather central. Nothing can guarantee that some quite unforeseen event might not impel the nuclear powers into a war with each other which they do not want. There have been enough unexpected political and military events in the last few years (e.g. the Iranian Revolution, the shooting down of KAL007) to demonstrate that the future is, in a fundamental sense, unknown. Given this basic ignorance, there is nothing to say that servants of governments which target their deterrent weapons on cities will not one day find themselves receiving orders to do the unthinkable and, by the standards of common Christian morality, the irredeemably wicked. Weighing up consequences is a necessary part of anyone's decision-making, but it is only possible within a framework of already accepted goals, virtues and prohibitions. We are not sufficiently in control of the future to operate such a method without being firmly grounded in a tradition which puts these things first. Nuclear deterrence explicitly disregards the traditional goals and pro-hibitions that Western society has received from its traditions. It does this in order to exercise a control over the future which has no reality. This attempt to control the future by manipulating ultimate forces is another mark of idolatry.

Some other method of moral discernment is needed which is more suitable to the matter in hand. If we are going to let philosophy play an important part in our moral decisions it must be a philosophy which is guided by the goals and limits of morality itself and not one which is derived from some other field of human affairs which itself should be subject to moral limitations.

4. *The relevance of tradition*

A number of moral philosophers have recently turned their attention to tradition itself as an indispensable factor in all genuine morality.[7] Tradition, once seen as the enemy of reason, has now become a respectable topic for rational analysis. Reasoning alone cannot be a source of moral knowledge. It can only be of use within a context of community life and tradition which transmits information about what virtues are to be practised, what values aimed for, what evils to be avoided at all cost. Without this shared knowledge to work on it can produce any result or none, depending only on the preferences of the powerful. Consequently, the power of modern states, steamrolling over human rights and ready to massacre the innocent for the cause of security, can only effectively be resisted by those who can call on the resources of a tradition of practical wisdom which is the possession of a community which transcends state boundaries – such as a church.

Christian ethics is distinctive and particular to the Christian community and its traditions, because all genuine morality has this particularist quality. But a tradition, when it is alive, is far from being merely a state of mindless conformity to a set of rules. It is more like a continuous or sporadic argument about how certain fundamental values are to be embodied in the changing conditions of life. The better understanding of tradition that is now available to us is far removed from the notion of an unalterable deposit of rules without any rational basis, which it often appears to be in the minds of both fundamentalists and those who oppose reason to tradition. According to MacIntyre, a living moral tradition is an historically extended, socially embodied argument: an argument precisely in part about the goods which constitute that tradition.[8] So the justice, the charity, the peace-making – or any other of the key practices which constitute the tradition of Christian virtues – are subject to arguments about what they are, and about how, precisely, they are to be realized now in the social/political conditions of the present, which are so different from what Christians experienced in the past. Any authentic Christian morality has to learn from the past in order to face conditions that Christians of the past never dreamed of.

The centuries-old teachings of the church on peace, war and social justice are prime examples of this. Their roots lie in the Hebrew scriptures. The Bible does not simply tell us to be just, to be peaceful, to be 'good' and then leave us with nothing but the reason of the experts – the generals, the politicians or the economists – to work out some 'natural law' solutions to the question of content. It actually gives us a revelation, a positive statement, about which ones – among the various conflicting notions of justice and peace – are in accordance with God's purpose for a nation of free people. Thus we can say with confidence that a view of justice which puts the needs of the weak and disadvantaged at the centre is compatible with revelation in a way that a view of justice putting contract and competitive inequality at the centre is not.[9] And we can say that a view of peace which sees it founded upon just relations and self-determination is central to our biblical tradition in a way that a view of peace which sees it as order imposed by force from above is not. According to the tradition, certain views about these things are ruled out. They belong to other gods, not to the God of Abraham, Isaac and Jacob – or of Isaiah, Jeremiah and the writers of Leviticus and Deuteronomy, or of Jesus, or the Christian martyrs. Even though it is not simple to apply and although it needs a great deal of knowledge from other sources, there is an authentic, scripture-based approach to many of the issues of poverty and justice which agitate present-day British society.

5. *God and security in the Hebrew scriptures*

Recent work on war and violence in the Hebrew scriptures has produced some important results for the debate about national security in Christian societies. Real theological thought about security originates in the prophetic project of the Old Testament writings. The prophets were, originally, indispensable participants in the business of war-making and national security.[10] But the reactions of some of the prophets of YHWH to the wars of Israel and Judah completely transformed the idea of these things which was commonly held among the nations of the ancient Near East.

It is not possible to do anything more than summarize conclusions here.[11] What pre-exilic Israel shared with the surrounding nations was the notion of war as a religious activity. It was begun by command of the gods, omens were taken, prophets were engaged to curse the enemy, sacrifices were made, the warriors were purified, and the gods were thanked for victory. Against some permanent enemies, victory culminated in *herem* – the sacrificial destruction of everything captured, including the people who would otherwise be used as slaves. Where Israel differed from its neighbours was in relating its wars to the historical experience of the Exodus, when YHWH fought for his people against a vastly superior enemy, and in its refusal to adopt the model of sacred kingship which operated among the nations. The exceptional prophets of YHWH continually kept the remembrance of these traditions alive in the face of other tendencies. This meant that in some respects Israel remained politically 'backward' in its ideology of war, in its social structure and in its military methods. But in doing so it managed to preserve the memory of a justice and a peace that the royal states around them had little time for.

Contrary to the ideology of other nations, Israel's sacred writers would never agree that Israel's wars were the king's wars – despite the attempts of the kings from David onwards to make them appear so. They were YHWH's wars on behalf of his people. In keeping with the Exodus tradition, it was YHWH's miraculous power that was to deliver Israel, not the power of a sacred king with his standing armies and his modern weapons. The power was ultimately with God, not with superior weapons. There was consequently a repudiation – very widespread in the Hebrew scriptures – of 'chariots and horses', which were the military technology characteristic of the divinized state power at that time. This amounts to an ideological difference between wars in which YHWH is the leader and wars in which a king is the leader. It was Saul's failure to recognize this distinction in his violation of the *herem* which began his downfall (I Sam. 15).

The repudiation of war as something entirely under the king's control was paralleled by a critique of the social effects of kingships (I Sam. 8). Kingship which simply reproduced the conditions of slavery under which Israel lived in Egypt was constantly opposed. There was a permanent attachment to equality among the men of Israel, which would not allow the king to become a divine figure set at the apex of a social pyramid or the owner of the whole land, as in other nations. The message was that God alone is sovereign – he is not, like the idols of the nations, a part of the royal power show. Israel's understanding of *shalom*, peace, is egalitarian: it is the possession of those freed from slavery. In its wars against the nations, Israel's continues to struggle against fresh royal domination. The history of the kingship in Israel is the history of the failure to produce this *shalom* because of desertion of YHWH through copying the ways of the neighbouring kingdoms with their standing armies, all-powerful divine kings, their accumulations of wealth, latest military hardware, subservient prophets and diviners, alliances with powerful neighbours through outside marriages – all the things that 'Moses' in Deuteronomy tells the kings of Israel not to do (Deut. 17.14–20).

The prophets opposed idolatry along with the wrong kind of kingship. The worship of idols puts national security as the rulers understand it at the centre, and tries to manage the cult to produce it, instead of submitting to the rule of God. The YHWHism of the prophets however, puts justice at the centre and declares the security of the nation to be conditional upon its practice. The unjust society becomes indefensible in both a moral and a military sense. Consequently, as Israel became like the other Near Eastern states, the prophets declared that YHWH's war was directed against Israel herself (for instance, Amos 3 and 4).

The refurbishment of the holy war tradition as we find it in the book of Deuteronomy was meant to restore YHWH's sovereignty over Israel's wars after generations of apostasy and failure. But it was too late. Israel – the kingdom of Judah, to be precise – could not maintain its freedom for ever as a small state with a backward military tradition. There came a time – namely the time of Jeremiah, at the end of the monarchy – when all the small nations were threatened by the great militaristic empires and when a new understanding of freedom had to be developed. Fighting with YHWH's help against the chariots and horses of small local kingdoms was one thing. The struggle against the great predatory powers such as Assyria and Babylon was quite another: it did not permit such victories, and Israel had to find a new way of survival which dispensed altogether with the need for kings, armies and 'national security'. It was under these circumstances that the universal mission of Israel began to be worked out by the prophets of the Exile.

In the writings of the New Testament the prophetic teaching about security and God's sovereignty is not abandoned in favour of a totally other-worldly spirituality, but developed to suit the special circumstances of the infant church in the Roman State. There is not a single view about this in the New Testament writings because there was not a single social background or single theology for the writers. Nevertheless, it is possible to identify elements of a distinctive Christian approach to justice, peace, security, which continue the Old Testament prophetic teaching. Everywhere in the New Testament is the imprint of the tension, or outright conflict, between Christian worship of the true God and the demands of the idolatrous Roman State.[12]

6. *How does God act in the world?*

One cannot maintain there is a simple parallel between what God required of ancient Israel and what he requires of modern nations. There is no question of any other nation being chosen by God in the sense that Israel was chosen. The revelation is on a deeper level. What we have here is the beginning of the politico-religious question that has constantly occupied the political thinkers of Christianity – does God work his will for the human race through 'churches', in exile so to speak, or through states? Is it the life of the faithful – usually obscure and marginalized and without power – in which God's action in the world is to be found, or in the doings of the powerful on the bright stage of history? Is it the peace that is lived in the community of disciples which corresponds to the peace of the kingdom, or is it the 'peace' that is achieved through acts or threats of annihilation, crushing all opposition? In so far as the church may always be called upon to resist the religious pretentions and idolatrous tendencies of states, the authentic answer lies nearer the first alternative than the second. The entire New Testament is a witness to this answer. There – whatever the attitude of the different writers to the Roman State – it was in the obscure Christian communities living a life of 'exile' that God's purpose was being fulfilled: not, that is, on the grand stage of history occupied by the Roman State. It is the Magnificat which expresses this best of all – all the more strikingly, for being in a gospel which otherwise treats Roman officials with respect.

But conflict – even though unsought by Christians – was inevitable. No more than Jesus did they constitute a political force or threaten armed subversion, yet they were soon treated as if they were a special threat to the security of the Roman state. It is worth asking why this was so. Although it is not easy to spell out the answer in terms that are intelligible in the twentieth century, it certainly had much to do with the Christians' resistance to idolatry. This was not simply a 'religious' matter, at least not in the sense that we have come to understand religion. Our understanding of religion as a private concern which the state has no right to interfere with was unknown to Christians and pagans alike. When the Christians were commanded to burn incense to the Emperor, the Roman officials were not interfering in their private lives but testing their ultimate loyalty to Roman society. Sacrificing to the gods was an integral part of it. The issue of eating meat offered to idols – clearly a very significant one in the churches of Asia Minor, judging by Paul's letters and the Book of Revelation – had the same implications. It chiefly affected poor Christians, who could not afford to eat any other kind of meat, and it raised suspicions of radical dissent and alienation from society. Christians were called 'atheists' and 'enemies of the human race', because of their repudiation of the ordinary rituals which guaranteed the security of the Empire.[13] Their perverse loyalty to a criminal executed by the Roman state for sedition was further evidence of their hostility to ordinary society.

None of this was an obstacle to a positive attitude towards the officials of the Roman State in the tradition of Paul in Romans 13. The opposition was at a deeper level. All authority may well be from God, but when the state oversteps its proper limits it becomes mere power without authority. Then its latent opposition to the Christian gospel becomes manifest. Paul's teaching was repeated by Irenaeus who, in 177 CE, narrowly escaped martyrdom at Lyons. In his view political authority was a necessary evil brought about by human sin. As such it was part of God's plan for the restraint of the devil, but it could serve the devil itself by acting illegally and tyrannically. There were strict limits to obedience.[14] This teaching had a profound effect on the political theology of the Western church.

7. *The situation of the churches today*

If present day states are idolatrous in respect of their national security policies, Christian citizens cannot escape the situation by a retreat from politics into religion, as many are now trying to do. It is not possible to abstract ourselves from the idolatrous conduct of the state when everything we do – our family lives, our jobs, our religious worship – is all secured within the confines of the nuclear threat. We exist by grace of it. This has inescapable consequences for Christian worship in a nuclear state. Once the practice of the state comes to be understood as idolatrous, it puts in question all worship and religious life which takes place under its protection. Genuine non-idolatrous worship cannot then take place without the church putting itself in opposition to the very protection which the state provides. We cannot pretend that the doings of the state are purely secular, following their own autonomous laws, while religion pursues its own objectives in its own sphere: when the very pursuit of those objectives must take place within a 'peace' that is secured by an idolatrous practice.

In at least one significant respect the situation of Christians today differs profoundly from that of the first Christians. We live in a post-Christian, not a pre-Christian world. In a state like Britain there is still inexhaustible respect for Christians who know their place and stay in it. Christians, like some colonized peoples, are free to live their own lives, follow their own customs so long as they stick to the 'reservations' set aside for them by the states to which they belong. Whatever they do within these reservations cannot have the slightest effect on what the states do. Consequently, the evil of nuclear preparations cannot effectively be opposed from a position 'inside' the churches. The most faithful performance of the sacraments, the most inspired preaching of the word or the warmest spiritual fellowship among the congregations will not make any difference to the false religion which exists outside, within whose 'protection' they are forced to operate. It is only by risking their respectability, by coming out of the reservation to preach the gospel in the public places that any challenge at all can be made.

Postscript: 'Peacemaking in a Nuclear Age'[1]

Alan Race

What has theology to do with making peace between nations? In one sense nothing at all: theology is not prescriptive for politics, and military strategy and international relations do not need to refer to theology for guidance or support. At another level, it has everything to do with peace between nations, for the language of peace itself is loaded with assumption and meaning that often extends beyond the supposed pragmatic form of military planning and political manoeuvre, to embrace ethical codes and a certain view of what is worth defending in a society. Peace is too precious to be left to the politicians alone.

In 1983 the General Synod of the Church of England debated the controversial report *The Church and the Bomb*, amid a blaze of publicity and in an atmosphere of neurotic East-West tension. The report had achieved publicity mainly for its alignment of the rejection of the doctrine of mutual nuclear deterrence with the support for unilateral nuclear disarmament by Britain. Both points were in opposition to current government policy. Other reports of church bodies at that time, if not so stridently critical of the doctrine of deterrence, were distancing themselves from it. Most notable in this respect was the Pastoral Letter on War and Peace in the Nuclear Age of the American Catholic Bishops, *The Challenge of Peace*, which talked of the morality of nuclear deterrence as valid only if it was a demonstrable step on the road to disarmament.[2]

The main proposals of *The Church and the Bomb* were rejected

169

by the Anglican Synod. Five years later another working party has produced the second report *Peacemaking in a Nuclear Age*, without a blaze of publicity and against a very different East-West atmosphere. For the moment, we no longer have the 'evil empire' speeches from the United States, nor the closed-door defensiveness of the Soviet Union. Moreover, the nuclear deterrence debate in the church has reached a stand-still, with those in favour and those against unable to find much common middle ground. The time seems ready for a different approach and a new look at the churches' involvement in the politico-nuclear debate. Does the new report help us to find a role for theology or the churches?

The intention of the report is to shift the emphasis away from the debate about nuclear deterrence, towards concern with the political and the theological rather than the militarist and ethical dimensions of a nuclear-armed world. Whether that is a legitimate division of responsibilities for both 'theology' and 'politics' is a moot point. But as 'theology' is so often accused of irrelevance when it comes to the arena of international relations, the promise of theological debate in the context of the 'real world' is presumably to be welcomed. Yet it is far from clear how the connections are to be made, and the report itself deserves only limited applause in achieving its goal. The connections it makes seem more exhortatory than actual.

The reasons for this spring not only from the extremely difficult nature of the task, but also from the way in which the report sets out its material. Two chapters outlining the Christian understanding of peace and hope are followed by substantial sections which examine the international relations context surrounding the whole nuclear debate, and a final chapter looks at how Christian groups and churches might be involved in the issues. This leaves the impression that theology functions either as a preface to a discussion of international relations which is then pursued in its own terms, or as a poor follow-on, blessing the limited moves that are being made – say, in arms control or human rights – towards decreasing the tension between the superpowers and their allies since the end of the Second World War and the rise of the Cold War.

This is not to say that the report does not set out some well-balanced views on a complex of issues, such as East-West perceptions, human rights, arms control, third world conflicts, détente, and so on. Such material will undoubtedly serve a major use in the coming debate, helping Christians and others to have some grasp of the world context in which the nuclear debate takes place. It should also help to overcome the feeling of paralysis that the problem is 'all too big' for ordinary citizens to enter into. Many will rightly see these sections as the report's strength. The discussion will not satisfy everyone, for it is not possible to be wholly objective, even when the report calls down a plague on both superpower houses. I notice, for example, that there is not much acknowledgment that it is the Western powers who have, on the whole, led the technological way in the nuclear arms race.

But my concern here is with the technological issues raised in the report. A further impression arises out of the arrangement of the material: 'theology as preface' is strong and visionary, while 'theology as follow-on' is weak and emasculated. The reasons for this draining away of theological strength as the report proceeds spring partly from the accommodation to secular powers (of which Roger Ruston speaks, above pp.144ff.), and partly from a failure to highlight the depth of the crisis in theology and the politics of defence, precipitated with the advent of nuclear weapons (of which Peter Selby speaks, above pp.29ff.). I wish to comment on each of these points.

Peacemaking in a Nuclear Age outlines three aspects of the Christian understanding of peace: *shalom* is the vision of a just and peaceful society under the rule of the Kingdom of God, a transformed world of physical and spiritual wholeness; *pax* is the absence of war, where degrees of coercion are also necessary for the sake of resisting domination by harmful forces; *inner serenity* is that peace of mind which an individual might achieve in relation to the God of peace. There are tensions between these three aspects of peace, the report says, but all are required in the task of peacemaking. Nevertheless it affirms priorities: while *shalom* defines the ultimate allegiance of Christian discipleship, it can only be approached via the conditions of *pax* and *inner serenity*. The report is then mainly concerned, in the context of relations between nations, with the first two dimensions of the Christian understanding of peace.

There is some slipperiness in the way the report speaks of the relations between these two aspects of peace. As it says, 'Until the Kingdom of God comes in its fullness, that is so long as God wills human societies to exist under sinful conditions, these two sets of claims will live in necessary tension with one another' (p.15). The priority of *shalom* thus remains for ever out of reach, leaving our task in the world as one of securing sufficient *pax* or 'absence of conflict', for life to be viable in an imperfect world. Securing an absence of conflict may indeed be all that can be achieved in a dangerous and exploitative world, but it is hardly all that needs to be said from a Christian perspective.

Between the concepts of *pax* and *shalom*, there is both continuity and discontinuity. On the side of continuity, it is a fair account of Christian involvement in peacemaking to view *shalom* as a goal and *pax* as potentially participating in it. There is nothing wrong in compromise between the ideal and the possible in a manifestly imperfect world. On the side of discontinuity, we must not forget the critique which *shalom* offers to *pax*, especially when Christians and theologians are drawn into the spell of international politics. In the report, the balance between compromise and critique, tips firmly in the former's favour.

This brings me to the second of my comments regarding the decay in theological strength as the report proceeds. While the report wishes to speak to and in the 'real world', it actually does not remind us *in any forceful way* of the 'real world' which the nuclear age represents: the nuclear overkill capacity, the power of the industrial-academic-military complex, the human and environmental effects of the use of nuclear weapons, the psychological damage to human minds living in the shadow of total threat, the massive investment in Star Wars and future weapons systems, e.g. Trident (a massive unilateral increase in nuclear destructive capacity). Without the full recognition of this context, the sense of *crisis* that has occupied many throughout the last decade is played down. While it is human beings who wage wars, the weapons and technology systems themselves cannot be discounted.

Responsibility for our world has passed into human hands in the sense that we no longer look to God to intervene to rescue us from disaster. The report acknowledges this last factor: 'For the first time, it is possible that relatively few human actions might eliminate all human life from the planet.' (p.30). But it does not see the theological implications this entails, particularly the question mark against any interpretation of the sovereignty of God which guarantees that 'all shall be well'. Though the report does not accept any optimistic account of God's providence, it also does not register fully the immense fragility of the world, once we take account of the threat under which we actually live.

The implications of all this for Christian peacemaking are far-reaching. In the context of the processes of seeking arms control, human rights, and détente – highly laudable aims in themselves – pursuing peace is dependent on some sense of durability in our world, some sense of underlying continuity under the umbrella of nuclear 'defence'. Yet it is precisely this sense of durability which is under threat, and which requires us to rethink the meaning of defence and any theology which may be related to it. Under such circumstances theology ought to place before us the real choice: either acquiescent and *pax*-minded co-operation with the philosophy of nuclear 'defence' and arms control, or Christian and *shalom*-minded resistance as a form of radical response to the changed conditions in a nuclear world.

Given the deficiency both in tackling the theological problems of the nuclear age and in underplaying the difference which the weapons themselves make in the equation, it is small wonder that the visionary peace of *shalom* is replaced by the myopic peace of *pax*.

This is made even clearer in the report's chapter on nuclear deterrence, where visionary theology is squeezed out in the never-ending quest to justify the conditional intention to hold the planet to ransom. Knowing that for nuclear deterrence to be credible it must involve the willingness to use nuclear weapons, the report seeks to circumvent this moral awkwardness by a final appeal to the Just War tradition, and an argument about balancing the risk of having a credible threat against an incredible fear if we have too many weapons making the threat. In the first place, it is a sign of desperation to employ the Just War principles of proportion and discrimination in the nuclear age. They ceased really to have any relevance since the introduction of aerial bombing. In the second place, there is no real difference between the two kinds of risk being proposed: what is sufficient to threaten *unacceptable* damage is also sufficient to fuel fear.

Does the new report help? The answer is 'yes' if you believe all is well, now that the superpowers are talking to one another and that we will learn to control our own technological hubris, and that theology can be adapted to suit your own purposes. It is 'no' if you believe that behind the odd breakthrough in East-West relations nothing much fundamentally has changed, that the nuclear arms race has achieved a life of its own, and that theology deserves a better visionary profile than what has been offered here. This has been, at least, the intention of the lines of exploration pursued by the authors in this collection of essays.

Notes

1   Introduction   *Alan Race*

1. *The Observer*, 1 January 1978.
2. 1946, cited in O. Nathan and H. Norden (eds), *Einstein on Peace*, Schoken Books 1960.
3. Cited in Marc Ian Busch, *The Little Black Book of Atomic War*, Dell Publishing, New York 1983, p. 20.
4. Cf. J. Garrison, *The Darkness of God: Theology after Hiroshima*, SCM Press 1982; G. Kaufman, *Theology for a Nuclear Age*, Manchester University Press 1985; S. McFague, *Models of God: Theology for an Ecological and Nuclear Age*, Fortress Press and SCM Press 1987.
5. Kaufman, op. cit., p. ix.
6. D. Forrester, 'Defining the Problem', *Ethics and Defence*, ed. H. Davis, Blackwell 1986, ch. 2.
7. Ibid., p. 34.
8. For the ethical debate see for example: Church of England Working Party of the Board of Social Responsibility, *The Church and the Bomb*, Hodder & Stoughton 1982; F. Bridger (ed.) *The Cross and the Bomb*, Mowbray 1983; R. Gill, *The Cross against the Bomb*, Epworth 1984; J. Gladwin (ed.), *Dropping the Bomb*, Hodder & Stoughton 1985; P. J. Murnion (ed.), *Catholics and Nuclear War: A Commentary on the Challenge of Peace. The US Catholic Bishops' Pastoral Letter on. War and Peace*, Chapman 1983 (includes the Catholic Bishops' letter).
9. *Peacemaking in a Nuclear Age*, CHP 1988.
10. See Elizabeth Templeton, 'Power and Powerlessness', *Ethics and Defence*, ch. 14, and also the essay by Roger Ruston in this collection.

2   Theology in a Nuclear Context   *Jonathan Draper*

1. G. Kaufman, *Theology For A Nuclear Age*, Manchester University Press 1985, p. 7.
2. J. Garrison, *The Darkness of God: Theology after Hiroshima*, SCM Press 1982, pp. 72ff.
3. Ibid., p. 3, my emphasis.
4. R. J. Schreiter, *Constructing Local Theologies*, Orbis Books and SCM Press 1985.
5. T. Balasuriya, *Planetary Theology*, Orbis Books and SCM Press 1984.
6. L. Boff, *Ecclesiogenesis*, Orbis Books and Collins 1986, p. 18.
7. Ibid., p. 18.
8. Kaufman, op. cit., pp. 8–9.
9. J. M. Soskice, *Metaphor and Religious Language*, Clarendon Press 1985.

Notes

10. Kaufman, op. cit.; Garrison, op. cit.; S. McFague, *Models of God*, Fortress Press and SCM Press 1987; J. Moltmann, *God in Creation*, SCM Press 1985. Another, perhaps even more impressive approach to this set of questions, comes from the Japanese theologian Kazo Kitamori (*The Theology of the Pain of God*, John Knox Press and SCM Press 1965), who took seriously the realities of the context in which he lived in what is arguably the world's darkest hour yet, the Second World War, and developed an understanding of the 'pain-love' of God. God engaged in, indeed tormented by the pain of God's own love for the world and the world's agony. God is understood here as seeking humanity and seeking in humanity, with humanity, that co-operative love which will bring the world to peace – a godly community in harmony with God, each other and the world.

11. Grace Jantzen, *God's World, God's Body*, Darton, Longman & Todd 1984.

12. Moltmann, op. cit., p. 17.

3 Apocalyptic – Christian and Nuclear   *Peter Selby*

1. This essay is adapted from a paper given at Trevelyan College, University of Durham, on 26 January 1983, in a series of seminars on *The Church and the Bomb*, the report of a working party under the chairmanship of the Bishop of Salisbury, published by Hodder & Stoughton 1982. It first appeared in *The Modern Churchman*, Vol. XXVI, No. 2, 1984, and is reproduced here with the permission of the editor.

2. J. Garrison, *The Darkness of God: Theology after Hiroshima*, SCM Press 1982, pp. 63–66.

3. *The Church and the Bomb*, pp. 106–7.

4. J. Schell, *The Fate of the Earth*, Cape/Picador 1982.

5. I am indebted to Dr H. H. Guthrie for his exegesis of the myth of the deluge.

6. *The Fate of the Earth*, pp. 159–60.

4 Discerning the 'Abomination of Desolation'   *Christopher Rowland*

1. Klaus Wengst, *Pax Romana and the Peace of Jesus*, SCM Press 1987, p. 133.

5 The Armageddon Scenario   *Mark Corner*

1. Gore Vidal, *Armageddon?: Essays 1983–1987*, Deutsch 1987. The article entitled 'Armageddon?' was reproduced in *The Observer* on 15 November 1987.

2. Hal Lindsey's bestseller *The Late Great Planet Earth*, was published in the United States by Zondervan in 1970. For a review of the 'Armageddon' theorists and a short bibliography at the end of the article see Roger Ruston, 'Apocalyptic and the Peace Movement', *New Blackfriars*, Vol. 67, no. 791, May 1986.

3. Useful in this context is Norman Cohn's *The Pursuit of the Milennium*, M. T. Smith and Paladin 1970.

4. Eric Fromm, *The Fear of Freedom*, Ark Paperbacks 1984.

5. The subject is discussed in James Thompson's *Psychological Aspects of Nuclear War*, British Psychological Society 1985. See especially ch. 2, 'Reactions to Disaster'.

6. Vidal, op. cit., p. 114.

7. Philip Berryman, *Liberation Theology*, Tauris 1987, p. 42. For interesting comments on liberation theology as enabling for First as well as Third World countries, see Richard Schaull, *Heralds of a New Reformation*, Orbis Books 1984.

7   Prayer in the Belly of the Beast   *Terry Tastard*

1. The only works I know dealing directly with spirituality and nuclear issues are Mark Mills-Powell, *Praying in the Shadow of the Bomb*, Grove Books 1984; Kenneth Leech, 'The Shape of Babylon', *Can Spirituality Be Taught?* ed. Jill Robson and David Lonsdale, ACATE/BCC 1987; Jim Wallis, 'The Work of Prayer', *Waging Peace*, ed. Jim Wallis, Harper & Row 1982.

2. Gordon Wakefield (ed.) *A Dictionary of Christian Spirituality* SCM Press 1983 p. v.

3. Lesslie Newbigin *The Other Side of 1984*, WCC 1983, p. 1.

4. For a discussion of how nuclear fears are both widespread and repressed, and of the impact this has, see Dorothy Rowe, *Living with the Bomb*, Routledge & Kegan Paul 1985, especially chs 1–3.

5. David McLellan (ed.), *Karl Marx: Early Texts*, Blackwell 1979, p. 135.

6. Notably Gerard W. Hughes, *God of Surprises*, Darton, Longman & Todd 1985; and Charles Elliott, *Praying the Kingdom*, Darton, Longman and Todd 1985. For a similar approach, but without the same prominent concern for social issues, see Anthony de Mello, *Saddhana*, Anand Press 1978.

7. Sallie McFague, *Models of God*, Fortress Press and SCM Press 1987, p. 13.

8. Joanna Rogers Macy, *Despair and Personal Power in the Nuclear Age*, New Society Publishers 1983, p. 140.

9. Wendell Berry, 'Defence of the Realm', *Resurgence*, Jan/Feb 1987, No. 120, p. 5.

10. Janet Morley, *All Desires Known*, jointly published by the Movement for the Ordination of Women and Women in Theology 1988, p. 26.

11. Walter Brueggemann, *The Prophetic Tradition*, Fortress Press 1978, p. 49.

12. Grace Mojtabai, *Blessed Assurance*, Secker 1987, p. 47.

13. Brueggemann, op. cit., p. 63.

14. Brueggemann, op. cit., p. 21.

15. Gregory Baum, *The Social Imperative*, Paulist Press 1979, p. 129.

8   Affirming all our Humanity   *Donald Evans*

1. This essay is also to appear in the United States as a contribution to *Spirituality Today*.

2. Dorothy Dinnerstein, *The Mermaid and the Minotaur*, Harper & Row 1976.

9 A Nuclear End: Would God ever let it happen?   *Brian Russell*

1. See for example O. C. Quick, *Doctrines of the Creed*, Nisbet & Co. 1938, pp. 132f. and pp. 184f., and *Doctrine in the Church of England, the 1938 Report*, reprinted by SPCK 1982, pp. 55f. and 74f. Jürgen Moltmann, *The Trinity and the Kingdom of God*, SCM Press 1981, sums up the English contribution on pp. 32–42.

2. See for example W. H. Vanstone, *Love's Endeavour, Love's Expense, The Response of Being to the Love of God*, Darton, Longman & Todd 1977, and *The Stature of Waiting*, Darton, Longman & Todd 1982; A. R. Peacocke, *Creation and the World of Science*, Clarendon 1979, and *Intimations of Reality, Critical Realism in Science and Religion*, University of Notre Dame 1984; John Macquarrie, *In Search of Deity, An Essay in Dialectical Theism*, SCM Press 1984; J. V. Taylor, *The Go-Between God, The Holy Spirit and the Christian Mission*, SCM Press 1972; and Jürgen Moltmann, *The Crucified God*, SCM Press 1974, *The Trinity and the Kingdom of God*, SCM Press 1981, and *God in Creation, An Ecological doctrine of creation*, SCM Press 1985. Also Maurice Wiles, *God's Action in the World*, SCM Press 1986.

3. See for example Jürgen Moltmann, *The Church in the Power of the Spirit*, SCM Press 1977, pp. 189ff.

4. Aquinas, *Summa Theologiae*, la, 19. 2.

5. Aquinas, *Summa Theologiae*, 5, 22 and 23; and 11, 83. 1.

6. See Don Cupitt, *Taking Leave of God*, SCM Press 1980, *The World to Come*, SCM Press 1982, and *Only Human*, SCM Press 1985, as well as my 'With Respect to Don Cupitt', *Theology*, Vol. LXXXVIII, January 1985, pp. 5–11.

10 Theodicy and the God of Hiroshima   *Elisabeth Holditch*

1. K. Surin, *Theology and the Problem of Evil*, Blackwell 1986, p. 52.

2. S. Milgram, *Obedience to Authority*, Tavistock 1974.

3. E. Schillebeeckx, *Christ: The Christian Experience in the Modern World*, SCM Press 1980, p. 699.

4. D. Soelle, *Suffering*, Darton, Longman & Todd 1975, p. 43.

5. F. Sontag, 'Anthropodicy and the Return of God', *Encountering Evil* ed. S. T. Davis, T. & T. Clark 1981, p. 145.

6. J. Yung Lee, *God Suffers with Us*, Nijhoff 1974, passim.

7. M. Wiles, *God's Action in the World*, SCM Press 1986, p. 48.

8. C. Hartshorne, *Aquinas to Whitehead: Seven Centuries of Religion*, cited in J. Garrison *The Darkness of God: Theology After Hiroshima*, SCM Press 1982, p. 40.

11 Cosmic Purpose in Evolutionary Perspective   *J. MacDonald Smith*

1. R. Bertell, *No Immediate Danger*, Women's Press 1985.

2. Rustum Roy, *Experimenting with Truth*, Pergamon 1981.

3. F. Capra, *The Tao of Physics*, Bantam 1977.

4. A. Flew, *God and Philosophy*, Hutchinson 1969, p. 69.

5. J. MacDonald Smith *Church Quarterly Review*, Oct/Dec, 1965.

6. For this reference and the mention of Mary Hesse in this paragraph see, A. R. Peacocke, *Creation and the World of Science*, Oxford University Press 1979, pp. 19ff.

7. K. Popper, *The Logic of Scientific Discovery*, Hutchinson 1969, p. 111.

8. J. Huxley, Hardy and Ford, *Evolution as a Process*, Allen & Unwin, 1954, p. 13.

9. J. Monod, *Chance and Necessity*, Collins 1972.

10. Wigner, *The Logic of Personal Knowledge*, Routledge & Kegan Paul 1961.

11. Peacocke, op. cit., pp. 101ff.

12 Christian Involvement in an Interfaith Theology of Peacemaking
Alan Race

1. See: A. Kenny, *The Logic of Deterrence*, Firethorn 1985; J. Teichman, *Pacifism and Just War*, Blackwell 1986; Roger Ruston, 'Nuclear Deterrence and the Use of the Just War', *Objections to Nuclear Defence* ed. N. Blake and K. Pole, Routledge & Kegan Paul 1984; US Bishop's Pastoral Letter on War and Peace in the Nuclear Age, *The Challenge of Peace: God's promise and our response*, CTS/SPCK 1983.

2. The Pluralist hypothesis is explored more fully in: J. Hick, *Problems of Religious Pluralism*, Macmillan 1985; P. Knitter, *No Other Name?*, SCM Press 1985; P. Knitter and J. Hick (eds), *The Myth of Christian Uniqueness*, SCM Press 1988; A. Race, *Christians and Religious Pluralism*, SCM Press 1983; Wilfred Cantwell Smith, *Towards a World Theology*, Macmillan 1981.

3. *The Myth of Christian Uniqueness*, p. 190.

4. J. Schell, *The Fate of the Earth*, Picador 1982, p. 178.

5. K. Koyama, *Mount Fuji and Mount Sinai*, SCM Press 1984, pp. 255 and 128. Cf. Aloysius Pieris, 'Buddhism as a Challenge for Christians', *Christianity among the Religions*, ed. Hans Küng and Jürgen Moltmann, *Concilium* 183, T. & T. Clark 1984, pp. 60ff.

6. Rosemary Ruether, 'The Christian Roots of Anti-Semitism', *Theology and Racism 1* ed. K. Leech, from the Race, Pluralism and Community Group of the Board for Social Responsibility of the Church of England 1985, pp. 15ff.; Cf. 'Christology and Jewish-Christian Relations', *To Change the World*, SCM Press 1981.

7. Cf. R. Ruston and A. West, *Preparing for Armageddon: some theological advice for President Reagan*, Pax Christi, 1985; also the essay in this collection by Mark Corner, above pp. 52ff.

8. Arthur A. Cohen, *The Tremendum: a Theological Interpretation of the Holocaust* Crossroad, New York, 1981, p. 52. See also A. Cohen, 'In our Terrible Age: The *Tremendum* of the Jews', *The Holocaust as Interruption*, ed. E. Schüssler Fiorenza and David Tracy, Concilium 175, T. & T. Clark 1984. Cf. Rubinstein and J. Roth, *Approaches to Auschwitz*, SCM Press 1988.

9. *The Tremendum*, p. 76, parenthesis mine.

10. Margaret Chatterjee, *Gandhi's Religious Thought*, Macmillan 1983, p. 56.

Notes

11. This possibility is held by Peter D. Bishop, *A Technique for Loving: Non-violence in Indian and Christian Traditions*, SCM Press 1981, Ch. 11, Cf. Steven G. Mackie, 'Gandhi, Martin Luther King, Catonsville and Greenham Common', *Modern Churchman*, Vol. 25, No. 4, 1983.

12. *A Technique for Loving*, p. 91.

13   The Idols of Security   *Roger Ruston*

1. James R. Newman and Byron S. Miller, *The Control of Atomic Energy*, McGraw-Hill 1958, cited by Margaret Gowing, *Independence and Deterrence*, Vol. I, p. 321.

2. This method of moral argument is nowadays called *consequentialism* by philosophers, or more loosely, *utilitarianism*. For arguments against it as a general method in morals, see John Finnis, *Fundamentals of Ethics*, Oxford University Press 1983. For criticisms of its application to the deterrence debate, see John Finnis, Joseph M. Boyle Jr, and Germain Grisez, *Nuclear Deterrence, Morality and Realism*, Oxford University Press 1987.

3. Since the late fifties, Britain has followed the 'Moscow criterion' – it is said to be necessary for the British deterrent weapon to be able to penetrate the defences of Moscow. Deterrence is fully understood on all sides to depend upon the threat to civilian populations. See Finnis, Boyle and Grisez, op. cit. and Roger Ruston, *A Say in the End of the World*, Oxford University Press, forthcoming.

4. For instance, *Winning the Peace*, Joint Pastoral Letter of the French Bishops, paragraphs 26–30, in James V. Schall (ed.), San Francisco, Ignatius Press 1984.

5. In Geoffrey Goodwin (ed.), *Ethics and Nuclear Deterrence*, Croom Helm 1982, pp. 40–52.

6. Alasdair MacIntyre, *After Virtue*, Duckworth 1981, ch. 8.

7. For instance, Alasdair MacIntyre, *After Virtue*; Stanley Hauerwas, *The Peaceable Kingdom*, SCM Press 1983; Alan Donegan, *The Theory of Morality*, University of Chicago Press 1977.

8. MacIntyre, op. cit., ch. 14.

9. See Roger Ruston, 'A Christian View of Justice', *New Blackfriars*, August 1978, pp. 344–358.

10. See I Kings 22 for a story which illuminates the roles of both the 'court prophets' and the exceptional prophets of YHWH (in this case Micaiah ben Imlah) in the wars of the kings of Israel and Judah.

11. The following works are useful in this area: Roland De Vaux, *Ancient Israel*, Darton, Longman & Todd 1961, pp. 258–267; Milard C. Lind, *Yahweh is a Warrior*, Scottdale, Pennsylvania, Herald Press 1980; Paul D. Hanson, 'War and Peace in the Hebrew Bible', *Interpretation*, October 1984; Walter Brueggemann, *Revelation and Violence*, Marquette University Press, 1986.

12. See Klaus Wengst, *Pax Romana and the Peace of Jesus Christ*, SCM Press 1987 and Joseph Ratzinger, 'Biblical spects of the question of faith and politics', in *Church, Ecumenism and Politics*, St Paul Publications 1987, pp. 147–151.

13. See Robert L. Wilken, *The Christians as the Romans Saw Them*, Yale University Press 1984, pp. 117–125.
14. Irenaeus, *Adversus Haereses*, XXIV, 1–2.

14 Postscript: 'Peacemaking in a Nuclear Age'   *Alan Race*

1. Church of England General Synod Working Party Report, chaired by the Bishop of Oxford, *Peacemaking in a Nuclear Age*, CHP 1988.
2. *The Challenge of Peace: God's Promise and Our Response*, CTS/SPCK 1983.